Ken Gire: *Through the Eyes of Others*

"I'm just a writer; Ken is a real writer."

—MAX LUCADO

"If there is such a thing as the gift of writing, it is my opinion that Ken Gire has it. Creative, colorful, lucid, and easy to read, he has developed a firm grip on this elusive craft, much of which cannot be taught. In athletic terms, the man's a natural . . ."

—CHUCK SWINDOLL,
PASTOR, DTS CHANCELLOR

"My words of respect for the writings of Ken Gire could fill a legal pad. But short of that, let me just say he is one of the finest authors I know."

—LUCI SWINDOLL,
AUTHOR AND SPEAKER

"Ken Gire is a man who walks with God. He listens to his life and to the voice of God through all his experiences. As a result, Ken's gift of writing has had a profound impact on me and many others at our church. We reserve a special place on our bookshelves for the writings of Ken Gire, returning there often to be inspired by his powerful and honest use of story and image. When Ken has come to speak, his words have refreshed our souls, always providing us with a new way to look at the human condition and our quest to connect more deeply to God."

—NANCY BEACH, PROGRAMMING DIRECTOR
AND TEACHING PASTOR, WILLOW CREEK

"Ken Gire's pen is full of heaven's counsel. His writings always lead me to the Savior . . . lean in and learn."

—PATSY CLAIRMONT,
AUTHOR AND SPEAKER

"I eagerly await any book from the pen of Ken Gire."

—H. NORMAN WRIGHT, AUTHOR
AND PASTORAL COUNSELING

ANSWERING *the* CALL

ANSWERING *the* CALL

THE DOCTOR WHO MADE AFRICA HIS LIFE

THE REMARKABLE STORY OF
ALBERT SCHWEITZER

KEN GIRE

THOMAS NELSON
Since 1798

NASHVILLE   DALLAS   MEXICO CITY   RIO DE JANEIRO

Published in Nashville, Tennessee, by Thomas Nelson. Thomas Nelson is a registered trademark of Thomas Nelson, Inc.

Published in association with the literary agency of WordServe Literary Group, Ltd., 10152 S. Knoll Circle, Highlands Ranch, Colorado 80130.

Thomas Nelson, Inc., titles may be purchased in bulk for educational, business, fund-raising, or sales promotional use. For information, please e-mail SpecialMarkets@ThomasNelson.com.

Scripture quotations are taken from the King James Version.

Library of Congress Cataloging-in-Publication Data

Gire, Ken.
  Answering the call : the doctor who made Africa his life : the remarkable story of Albert Schweitzer / Ken Gire.
     pages cm
  Includes bibliographical references.
  ISBN 978-1-59555-079-8
1. Schweitzer, Albert, 1875-1965. 2. Missionaries, Medical--Gabon--Lambarene (Moyen-Ogooue)--Biography. I. Title.
  R722.32.S35G57 2013
  610.69092--dc23
  [B]

                                    2012036113

Printed in the United States of America
13 14 15 16 17 RRD 6 5 4 3 2 1

[Jesus] comes to us as One unknown, without a name, as of old, by the lake-side. He came to those men who knew Him not. He speaks to us the same word: "Follow thou me!" and sets us to the tasks which He has to fulfill for our time. He commands. And to those who obey Him, whether they be wise or simple, He will reveal Himself in the toils, the conflicts, the sufferings which they shall pass through in His fellowship, and, as an ineffable mystery, they shall learn in their own experience Who He is.

—ALBERT SCHWEITZER

Contents

CONTENTS

Author's Note

As you, the reader, make your way through this book, you will encounter a number of conversations between Albert Schweitzer and others, whose names you will become familiar with as you read. Unless otherwise indicated (with a numerical reference to a note), these conversations are for the most part surmised and assumed, based on research of Dr. Schweitzer's life through biographical and autobiographical works.

A couple of characters have been invented, although the majority of characters are factual. I have taken artistic license on wording and dialogue to illuminate certain facts and bring depth to the characters. My hope and intention are that this creativity gives you, the reader, the opportunity to not only read a book but also travel through time and enter the world of Albert Schweitzer and those whose lives weaved into his own.

Where text or dialogue has been taken from a particular source, a note is provided so that you may—if your interest in Albert Schweitzer grows as you read—delve further into his books and the writings of others about his life and work.

Chronology of Albert Schweitzer's Life

1875—Early Years

January 14, 1875. Albert Louis Philipp Schweitzer was born at Kaysersberg, Haute Alsace (then under German rule; today it is in the northeastern part of France on the German border), to Adele Schillinger Schweitzer and Louis Schweitzer, a Lutheran pastor.

1880–84. Educated at the local school in Günsbach, the village where he lived.

1884–85. Educated at Realschule at Münster, Upper Alsace.

1885–93. Educated at Gymnasium at Mulhausen, Upper Alsace.

October 1893. Went to Paris to study the organ with C. M. Widor, famous organist and writer on music.

November 1893. Began studies at the University of Strasbourg, where he studied theology, philosophy, and music theory.

April 1894. Entered the military in the 143rd Regiment. Service completed in April 1895.

1895—Twentieth Year

1896. Made commitment to serve humanity beginning at the age of thirty.

1896–99. Studied at the Sorbonne and the University of Berlin; also studied organ in Paris and Berlin. Began giving organ concerts.

Fall 1897. Wrote his thesis for his degree in theology, "The Idea of the Last Supper in Daniel Schleiermacher, Compared with the Ideas of Luther, Zwingli and Calvin."

May 6, 1898. Passed his oral and written exams before the faculty of theology. Subsequently, he received the Goll Scholarship in theology.

Summer 1898. Continued his studies in philosophy at the University of Strasbourg.

Fall 1898–spring 1899. Studied at the Sorbonne in Paris where he continued being mentored musically by Widor. Here he studied the original texts of Kant in order to trace the evolution of his thought.

March 12, 1899. Returned to Günsbach, where he worked on revising his manuscript on Kant.

April–July 1899. Continued his philosophical studies in Berlin as well as his studies in the organ.

July 1899. Returned to Strasbourg, where he successfully completed his exam in philosophy, earning him a PhD.

December 1899. Hired by St. Nicholas church in Strasbourg, where he worked on his thesis in theology on the historical origin of the Last Supper. At the end of December, he published the book *The Religious Philosophy* of Kant from the "Critique of Pure Reason" to "Religion within the bounds of Mere Reason."

July 15, 1900. Passed his second set of theological exams.

July 21, 1900. Graduated magna cum laude with a doctorate in theology.

September 23, 1900. Ordained as a minister at St. Nicholas church.

1902. Appointed privatdozent at the University of Strasbourg, where he gave lectures before the faculty on the structure of the gospel of John.

October 1, 1903. Received a permanent position as principal of the St. Thomas Theological Seminary.

1905—Thirtieth Year

January 14, 1905. At age thirty he made the decision to study medicine and go to Africa.

1906. Began medical studies at the University of Strasbourg.

June 18, 1912. Married Hélène Bresslau.

February 1913. Completed internship and received MD degree.

March 26, 1913. Left for Africa. Arrived at Lambaréné, Gabon, in French Equatorial Africa, where he built his first hospital.

1914. With the outbreak of WWI, French authorities considered him an enemy of the state. He was interned at Lambaréné but was allowed to continue practicing medicine.

1915—Fortieth Year

September 1915. After years of searching, he found the phrase "Reverence for Life" while traveling on the Ogowe River, which summed up his philosophy.

September 1917. The Schweitzers were transferred to France, where he and his wife were interned in prisoner-of-war camps at Garaison and later at St. Rémy. During that time he contracted dysentery.

July 1918. Returned to Alsace in poor health and learned that his mother had been killed.

January 14, 1919. Daughter Rhena, his only child, was born.

1919–23. He recovered his health, lectured widely in Europe, practiced medicine, gave organ concerts, preached, wrote, and published, including the two-volume *Philosophy of Civilization*.

February 1924. Wrote *Memoirs of Childhood and Youth.*

1924. Returned to Africa.

1925—Fiftieth Year

1926. He rebuilt hospital at new location.

1927–39. He made trips to and from Africa. Lectured widely and played organ throughout Europe to raise funds for his hospital.

1935—Sixtieth Year

February 1935. He returned to Africa for the fifth time.
September 1935. Returned to Europe to give concerts, raise money for the hospital, and make organ recordings of Bach.
February 1937. Returned to Africa for his sixth visit.
1939–44. Returned to Europe briefly for twelve days and then made his seventh trip to Lambaréné where he stayed during World War II. Mrs. Schweitzer joined him after her escape from Europe.

1945—Seventieth Year

1948. He returned to Europe for the first time since WWII.
July 1949. Made first and only trip to the United States.
October 1949. Took eighth trip to Africa.
June 1951. Returned to Europe to visit Mrs. Schweitzer and give concerts and lectures.
December 1951. Made his ninth trip to Africa.
July 1952. Returned to Europe to give lectures and concerts to raise money for his hospital.
December 1952. He made his tenth trip to Africa.
November 1953. Awarded the 1952 Nobel Peace Prize.
November 1954. Accepted the 1952 Nobel Peace Prize and delivered an address in Oslo, Norway.

1955—Eightieth Year

May 1955. Made his eleventh trip to Africa.

December 1955. Made his twelfth trip to Africa.

May 30, 1957. Hélène Schweitzer died in Switzerland.

December 4, 1957. Returned to Lambaréné for the thirteenth time. Brought his wife's ashes, which he buried on the hospital grounds.

1958–63. Worked for nuclear test ban treaty. A period of great expansion for his hospital.

May 6, 1963. Endorsed a US Senate bill to reduce laboratory animal experiments.

August 1963. Wrote to President Kennedy regarding the nuclear test ban treaty.

1965—Ninetieth Year

January 14, 1965. He celebrated his ninetieth birthday.

August 28, 1965. Designated his daughter to be administrator of the hospital.

September 4, 1965. Died at 10:30 p.m. in his bed at Lambaréné at age ninety.

Foreword

I still don't know whether I found Albert Schweitzer or he found me.

But I do know *when* we found each other.

I was living in Southern California at the time, and one night my oldest daughter asked me to drive her to a Bible study at a home in Orange County. We lived in Fullerton, not terribly far away but far enough that I didn't want to drive home just to turn around and drive back again to pick her up. So, after dropping her off, I looked for a place to park myself for a couple of hours.

I drove around the area and happened upon Chapman University where I saw a library. *Perfect*, I thought. Entering the small, cozy library was like falling into a tunnel that led to another time.

On the walls, staring down at me, were larger-than-life black-and-white photos of Schweitzer and his hospital in Lambaréné, Africa. He stood in them, a little hunched over, wearing baggy trousers and a loose-fitting white shirt. His face seemed an outcropping of weathered rock, jutting from some overgrown mountainside. A pith helmet shaded a shock of white hair and a wild but somehow distinguished moustache.

It was a little eerie, walking into this shrine, and a reverence filled the place, hushing everything inside me. Long glass cases enclosed bits and pieces of Schweitzer's life as if relics unearthed from an archeological dig.

A carefully folded white linen shirt, like the ones in the photographs, its weave thick and a little irregular.

A pair of gold-rimmed glasses.

A stout fountain pen.

A manuscript scrawled in faded cursive.

Early editions of his books.

A sheaf of his letters.

Medical paraphernalia, from stethoscopes to scalpels.

Before I knew it, two hours had passed, and I left to pick up my daughter. But something of Schweitzer left with me. Something of his life, his legacy, and the look on his careworn face followed me, shuffling a few feet behind me and just over my shoulder.

Over the years, every time I saw a book by him or about him, it snagged my attention. I stopped, leafed through it, and more often than not, ended up buying it and taking it home with me. The pictures were mesmerizing.

Him hand-feeding a pelican perched outside his hut.

Him examining an African with a protruding stomach.

Him directing the building of an addition to the hospital, doing much of the hard labor himself.

Him handwriting letters at the end of his day, a kitten curled near his hand.

Him folded over an old piano, playing Bach at night, his fatigued frame and arthritic fingers somehow enlivened by the music.

Him.

Who was he, this mysterious collection of mesmerizing images? Who was this man whose place in European academia was so secure? He had three doctorates. *Three.* In philosophy, theology, and medicine. He was also a well-respected author. On top of that, he was a concert organist and a world authority on Bach. Yet he left that ivory-towered world with its promises of fame and fortune, and he buried himself in the dark and dangerous jungles of Africa for a sweltering life of service to poor and needy people.

Why?

That is the mystery of his life, the mystery that haunted me that night in the library . . . and haunts me still.

1

The Tolling of the Bell at Lambaréné

As soon as man does not take his existence for granted, but beholds it as something unfathomably mysterious, thought begins.

—ALBERT SCHWEITZER

September 5, 1965

At 5:30 on a slow-stirring Sunday morning, the bell at the hospital in Lambaréné tolled. Soon the bell at the leper colony down the road joined it. Then tom-toms from surrounding villages relayed the sad news to the distant reaches of the jungle: "Papa Pour Nous is dead."[2]

The affectionate term was French for the fatherly doctor who had lived among the people of Gabon for the past fifty years, serving them with tireless devotion. Albert Schweitzer, Le Grand Docteur, had died quietly in his bed at 10:30 the night before, surrounded by a small circle of friends and coworkers, among them his daughter, Rhena.[3] Because the hour was late, it was decided to wait until morning to spread the news.

Now it was morning.

And the news spread from village to village until the normally teeming jungle seemed one long, heavy sigh.

Bare trails that crisscrossed and weaved as they branched off between an endless number of villages in West Gabon began to fill with people. Individuals, couples, and families from various tribes, of diverse backgrounds and a great range of ages, made their way toward the small riverside town of Lambaréné.

For some of those who gathered at his grave, their lives had begun at the Schweitzer Hospital; others' lives had been saved—or the life of a parent or child or spouse—through a timely operation and dedicated care. Some had received care for tumors, leprosy, ulcers, or life-threatening wounds. Now they gathered to sing, dance, and express grief in their own way to honor one who had honored them through the tireless devotion he had given for half a century.[4]

They were joined in one purpose: mourning the death of one whose selfless service had helped countless people in their region, the one who had committed to make his life his greatest sermon.

2

First Glimpses of a Foreign Shore

*The deeper we look into nature the more we recognize
that it is full of life, and the more profoundly we know
that all life is a secret, and we are all united to all this life.*
—ALBERT SCHWEITZER

First Glimpses of a Foreign Shore

Bells tolled from the church in the Alsatian village of Günsbach on a spring afternoon. Thirty-eight-year-old Albert Schweitzer and his wife, Hélène, stood in the sun-drenched station, waiting for the train that would take them to their destiny. A crowd of family and friends waited with them.

The bells belonged to the Lutheran church that Albert attended as a child, where his father, Louis, served as pastor, and his mother, Adele Schillinger Schweitzer, served faithfully by his side.

Thirty years ago those same bells rang at the same time of the year, also shortly before Easter. Young Albert and a friend had made slingshots, and the friend enticed him to shoot birds with him. Albert was an unusually sensitive child, and he hated the idea. But he was afraid the friend would laugh at him if he didn't. They approached a leafless tree, filled with birds, and each loaded his slingshot with a pebble. They crouched and took aim. All the while, Albert felt a stab of conscience and vowed to himself to miss. Just then the church bells rang, mingling with the songs of the birds. For Schweitzer, it was "a voice from heaven," calling to him. Immediately he put down the slingshot, shooed away the birds, and ran home.[1]

From that day on, he stopped fearing what other people thought of him, and his inner conviction about the sacredness of all life was fixed. At night, when his mother left the room after tucking him into bed and leading him in his evening prayers, he extended her petitions for people to include all living things—"and protect and bless all beings that breathe, keep all evil from them, and let them sleep in peace."[2] He did his part to be the answer to that prayer, protecting and blessing all living creatures any way he could. And he took that ethic with him to the savage jungles of Africa.

The tolling of those bells on that Lenten day was the first of many mystical experiences that shaped the course of Schweitzer's life. Now those bells fell silent. A gentle breeze brought the fragrances of spring from the Münster valley of Upper Alsace to the train station, where the agricultural smells of earth, grass, and flowers mingled with the industrial smells of steel, grease, and coal.

A whistle blew in the distance, causing everyone to crane their necks. The train rounded the bend, huffing plumes of smoke, its whistle blowing again as it chugged toward them. Brakes squealed as its massive wheels slowed, then stopped, a final whistle expending itself, as if from exhaustion.

While porters hefted their luggage onto the train, villagers stood around awkwardly, hands buried in their pockets, as if mourners at the funeral of someone who had died young, a life of promise denied him. Schweitzer was renowned as a lecturer, a writer, and a musician. People across Europe were still shaking their heads. So much talent, so much education, so much potential. It all seemed a waste. Why would such a gifted individual waste his life in a place that had been dubbed "the white man's graveyard"? Few believed it was even possible for foreigners to survive, much less remain healthy and robust, in the glaring sun and burning heat of Africa. And had he considered the hostility of tribesmen or the diseases that ravaged the jungle—unknown and unnamed, yet widely feared all the same?

A few final handshakes and hugs were exchanged, and more than a few fingers wiped cinders of sudden emotion from their eyes. Albert's father and mother hugged them both, his mother steeling herself against the rending moment.

Boarding the train, the Schweitzers hurried to the last coach for a final glimpse of the village, waving one last time to the life they were forever leaving behind. The train's whistle blew sharply as smoke belched from its stack. The engine strained, its lurch sending a jolt through the couplings between the cars. The Schweitzers steadied themselves on the railing as the train pulled away.

As Albert and Hélène waved good-bye, he blew a kiss to his mother.

It would be the last time he would see her.

Albert Schweitzer had earned three doctorates. The first in philosophy, in 1899. The second in theology, in 1900. The last one in medicine, in 1913. He had become an accomplished organist, a master of organ design and construction, the foremost authority in Europe on Johann Sebastian Bach, and a respected author. He spent the first three decades of his life devoted to philosophy and the arts. Yet at age twenty-one, he made the decision to give his life to the service of humanity once he was thirty. Soon after his thirtieth birthday, he began his medical training, exchanging his post as principal of the St. Thomas Theological College in Strasbourg for a seat as a student. During that time, he met Hélène Bresslau, and the two married on June 18, 1912. While he was in medical school, Hélène attended nursing school so that she could assist him in his work.

In February 1913, he completed his internship and received his MD. His training was over. His career as a humanitarian had begun.

Schweitzer was leaving behind a promising medical career, in Paris perhaps. A promising academic career, teaching at the university in Berlin or at the seminary in Strasbourg. A promising music career, touring Europe to keep the spirit of Bach alive through his organ concerts. And it was a sacrifice that only those closest to him knew how dear he held these talents. But he had other promises to keep. All other possibilities were now dead, taken away by train to be buried in a remote jungle in Africa.

Family, friends, and colleagues expressed their shock, disagreement, and wonder at his decision. Why would such a talented young man, with a promising career ahead and his choice of vocation, choose to leave it all behind? Were there not many others who could commit their lives to the service of mankind?

Perhaps the greater question was not who *could* but who *would*. Albert Schweitzer knew he must answer the call. The call that resounded in the hearts of many throughout the centuries. The call from one whose plea gave a haunting warning and an enduring promise: "If any man will come after me, let him deny himself, and take up his cross, and follow me. For whosoever will save his life shall lose it: and whosoever will lose his life for my sake shall find it" (Matt. 16:24–25).

He knew not on what adventures his answer to the call would take him, but for now, he knew where.

But who had even heard of Lambaréné?

As their ship dropped anchor off the shores of western Africa, the Schweitzers were transported to a riverboat named *Alembe*. The boat was flat and broad, its two paddlewheels slapping the water of the Ogowe River, as if to revive the sluggish currents. The Ogowe was a tangle of wide rivers that unraveled through the Congo, strands of it disappearing into the jungle so imperceptibly that it was difficult to tell where the water ended and the jungle started.

After a long ocean voyage and a terrifying pummeling from three days of an unrelenting storm, the slow waters of the Ogowe were a welcomed relief. As the pilot steered through the shallows, carefully avoiding sandbars, the Schweitzers stood at the railing as if children ferried into a dream more vivid than their schoolbooks could have captured or their childhood imaginations could have contained.

Roots overlapping each other on the banks. Clumps of papyrus. Strands of flowers laced through the brooding lushness. Palm trees standing tall and lean, a burst of green at each top. Giant ferns, fronding in all directions. The glistening back of a hippo breaking the surface of the yellow water, its snorty nostrils breaching for air. A rustling in the branches and a brightly plumed bird taking flight. In other branches, an argument of monkeys.

Late in the day, Schweitzer was talking with a French trader as they approached a clutter of tumbledown huts, the people lethargically moving about, if they moved at all.

"When I came here fifteen years ago," the trader said, "these places were all flourishing villages."

"And why are they no longer?" Schweitzer asked.

"L'alcohol," he said in a low voice.

The Europeans exported alcohol to Africa, along with various diseases that were previously unknown there. Schweitzer mused a moment, then said, "I wonder if the blessings we bring the natives outweigh the evils that go with them."

The trader shrugged his shoulders agnostically.

"What brings a man like you to Africa, educated, cultured? A man doesn't just turn his back on all that. Must be a story there somewhere."

"It's a *long* story," said Schweitzer, pulling a handkerchief from his back pocket.

"It's a long trip."

Schweitzer took off his pith helmet, then wiped his forehead with his handkerchief and blotted his neck. "My sympathy for the plight of the African came in my childhood, listening to my father's sermons. Once a month he spoke about missions. One Sunday he read from the memoirs of Eugene Casalis, a missionary to the Basutos. It made an impression. That was the first time the idea of becoming a missionary came to me. The next time was at Colmar. There was a monument, designed by Bartholdi, the sculptor who designed the Statue of Liberty in New York."

"I've been to Colmar," said the trader. "I know the monument."

"At its base was the sculpture of an African slave, leaning against it, strong and muscular, yet unmistakably sad. The misery of all of Africa was in his face. I felt it. And I never forgot it. Each time our family went back to Colmar, I went back to that man, resting at the base of that monument. And each time I felt the same misery.

"Then, later in my life, a parable of Jesus reached out to me, pressing its finger on my chest, the way that the prophet Nathan pressed his finger in David's chest with the parable he told."

"Which parable?"

"The one of the rich man and Lazarus, the poor beggar who had been dumped outside the rich man's gate. It seemed the parable had been spoken directly to us Europeans who had lived so prosperously, who had learned about diseases and how to treat them, about pain and how to alleviate it. Within our gates we had a wealth of knowledge, of procedures, of medicines. Outside our gates, in the colonies, sat Lazarus, the dark man, living in a dark continent, covered with sores and in agonizing pain. If we stay within our gates, we sin against the poor man who is suffering outside. Or so it seemed to me."[3]

"Why Lambaréné?" the man asked. "It's not even a city. Just swamp and jungle and a bunch of thatch huts. Lots of hardwood and a working mill down the way. A number of trading posts. Small mission with a school. Not much else, though."

"That's another story."

"Good," he said. "It will shorten the trip."

"I came across a magazine, of all things. I remember the day clearly. Morning. An autumn morning. 1904. And a shaft of sun coming in through the window of my room at the college. Falling on a magazine on my writing table. A green-covered magazine from the Paris Missionary Society. Casalis was one of their missionaries, and that is why I subscribed to it. Anyway, I picked it up, randomly opening it to a page that read, 'The Needs of the Congo Mission.' The article was by the president of the mission, Alfred Boegner. In the article he appealed to his readers, that some of them—in his own words—'on whom the Master's eyes already rested' would answer the call for this urgent work. 'Men and women who can reply simply to the Master's call, "Lord, I am coming."' The article concluded with the words, 'those are the people whom the Church needs.'[4]

"When I finished the article, I knew my search was over."

"All very mystical," the trader commented. "With your education, I figured you a rational man."

"God has joined faith and reason together harmoniously. It is man who puts them asunder. The more I understand Jesus, the more I am impressed by the way he combined faith and common sense. In the end, it seemed the most rational thing to do with my life, perhaps the *only* rational thing." Schweitzer gazed into the Frenchman's eyes. "And you. What brought *you* here?"

The man pointed to the dock on the river where a few Africans were stacking logs for export. "Timber. A *purely* rational decision, I assure you. I came for one reason only—to make money. Can't get more rational than that."

———

Five hours later, the slopes of Lambaréné slowly rose into view. The steamer blew its whistle, signaling the village to ready itself for the boat's arrival. The village suddenly swarmed with life and movement. Boys scurried into their canoes, paddling toward the boat to off-load its cargo. The boatmen stood, pushing their hollowed-out canoes with long poles.

One long pirogue approached swiftly, pushed along by a group of boys, singing cheerfully. A man stood in the stern of the boat, and he called out, "Good day, Dr. Schweitzer! I'm Mr. Christol from the mission."

Albert and Hélène greeted him, their voices soon drowned by the excited chatter among the boys on the boat.

"They just won the race," Mr. Christol volunteered, "against the older group. There they are, coming now."

Albert noticed another canoe approaching swiftly, a second group of boys paddling toward the ship.

"The prize for winning the race is escorting you to the mission."

A cheer rose from the boys as the couple gingerly lowered themselves into the boat, Albert gesturing to his wife that she sit in front of him to make sure she was safe.

They would have to wait a couple of weeks for the

seventy-some crates that held their medical equipment to finally reach the mission. Albert and Hélène took only their personal belongings and a few basic medical items.

"How far is it to the mission?" Albert looked warily at the yellow-tinged water lapping against the boat, which seemed to ride precariously low on the river.

"Andende is only an hour," Mr. Christol replied as the boys took command of the long slender poles and began to push once more. The second boat followed behind with their belongings.

"That is Mr. Ellenberger." Mr. Christol gestured toward the man overseeing the boys in the other boat. "We are teachers at the mission."

"Thank you for coming all the way for us."

Albert thought for a moment of the struggles he faced in gaining permission to join the mission as a doctor. It had been a challenge to gain acceptance from the traditional Paris Mission Society. It was widely known that Schweitzer's views on Christianity did not fit neatly into the dogmatic mold of Christianity during the early twentieth century. His point of view was that the truth of Jesus' teachings was strong enough to be subjected to thought and meditation, rather than mere belief. With the Sermon on the Mount, Jesus of Nazareth encouraged his followers to move forward in a spirit of righteousness—borne by the spirit—and to act upon their faith in a tangible manner. It was clear that Albert Schweitzer appreciated the history and teachings of the church, yet he considered those who followed Christ's "religion of love" with concrete service to mankind to be of greater importance than merely believing every doctrinal jot and tittle.

> Jesus . . . formulates no doctrine. He is far from judging any man's belief by reference to any standard of dogmatic correctness. . . .
>
> The religion of love taught by Jesus has been freed from any dogmatism which clung to it. . . . We are now at liberty to let the religion of Jesus become a living force in our thought, as its purely spiritual and ethical nature demands. . . . I am certain that truthfulness in all things belongs to the spirit of Jesus.[5]

The heartfelt greetings from the teachers began to alleviate his concerns about how the mission staff would react to his arrival. He was soon to discover that the issues of dogma, which appeared such a major factor to the committee in Paris, were not given the same consideration on the front lines. Here, if missionaries or teachers wished to be understood, they found it necessary to stick to the basic teachings of the gospel, God's love and mercy.

Schweitzer relaxed in the canoe and took in the view. As the glaring sun sank lower in the sky, the boats turned into a stream that branched from the main river Ogowe. One boy pointed toward a hill, alive with the light of the setting sun. White houses and buildings stood out among the trees like tiny white flowers peeking out from clusters of clover. *Among them,* surmised Albert Schweitzer, *will be a new hospital. Among them, our new home.*

Upon arriving at the Protestant Mission of the Paris Missionary Society, they were greeted by Mrs. Christol; the schoolmistress, Miss Humbert; a laborer named Mr. Kast; and some of the local people. The teachers led Albert and Hélène to their modest wooden house that had been decorated by the children with palm leaves and flowers. It stood on iron pilings that raised it twenty inches off the ground to keep the rushing water from washing away the foundation during the rainy season. A verandah ran all around the four small rooms that made up the house. They barely had time to unpack when the bell rang to signal evening prayers in the schoolroom. Albert and Hélène sat together on a wooden packing box outside, listening to the children's prayers. They held each other's hands as they listened, deeply moved.

After dinner, the children gave a musical program in honor of the doctor and his wife.

"I've never heard these verses before," Mrs. Schweitzer observed.

"Mr. Ellenberger composed these verses, especially for your arrival," came the touching reply.

When the festivities were over, the two were escorted back to their house, where, once they banished a few spiders and cockroaches, they stretched out on their beds. The sultry night air and the symphony of night sounds drifted in through their window. They were exhausted but exhilarated.

Africa, at last.

3

A Home Among the Hills

*Love cannot be put under a system of rules and
regulations. It issues absolute commands. Each of us must
decide for himself how far he can go towards carrying out
the boundless commandment of love.*

—ALBERT SCHWEITZER

1913–14

The dense forest, with its cacophony of primal noises, awoke Albert Schweitzer to his first morning in Africa. He stepped out on the wide verandah, surveying the scene before him. Their house was situated near the base of the sloping hill. Two hills stood on either side, with whitewashed buildings dotting the landscape. Beyond the hills flowed outlets of the Ogowe River, the main part of which streamed past the base of the hill. Dense foliage rose from the edge of the river, and its branches were teeming with vibrant life.

After breakfast, Dr. and Mrs. Schweitzer were invited to explore the grounds of the mission. They wore pith helmets as protection from the unrelenting glare of the sun. Beyond their house, nestled along the rising slope of the hill, were the missionaries' quarters. Small gardens had been cultivated outside the dormitory-like buildings and schoolrooms. Schweitzer noted the disrepair of many of the wooden structures, as well as the termite-ravaged porches and thatched roofs. At the edge of the buildings grew varieties of fruit—lemons, oranges, mangoes—cocoa plants, and palm trees.

"Where did these fruit trees come from?" Albert inquired, noting that they contrasted with the dense jungle that grew at the edge of the clearing, bordered by a natural fence of brush. He knew that fruit grew naturally in the jungle.

"They were planted by the first missionaries who came here, nearly forty years ago."

"There are no roads," observed Mrs. Schweitzer.

Mr. Christol pointed to the river. "That is the only road, highway, and avenue you will find. There is no other way to get through the jungle."

"How safe is it?" Dr. Schweitzer asked.

"Safe enough, I suppose. As long as you avoid the groups of hippopotami and watch out for crocodiles. You no doubt noticed we stayed closer to the bank than the center to avoid the rushing current. It's safer that way. The only problem is when poisonous snakes drop into the boat from the over-hanging tree branches."

"And is that a frequent occurrence?"

"It hasn't happened to me." He laughed good-naturedly. "Yet."

They had come to the end of their small-island tour, and an important question remained on Albert Schweitzer's mind.

"I didn't notice the building material."

"Material?"

"Yes, lumber, corrugated tin. The material I need to build the hospital. And where is it to be built?"

"I do not believe that has been decided yet."

Dr. Schweitzer was digesting this discouraging bit of information, mentally starting a list of the supplies he would need, most of which could be procured from the local lumber-yard. Timber was big business in Lambaréné; in fact, it was about the only business in Lambaréné. His train of thought was broken as a young mission student ran up, speaking excitedly.

"Doctor, Doctor, the patients have come. They are waiting for you!"

"Patients?" Schweitzer was clearly agitated. "I requested a three-week period upon arrival to ready the hospital."

Mrs. Schweitzer stepped close to his side. "Why don't we at least *see* the patients?"

Her smile convinced him of his already growing sense of duty. "Where are they?"

The student walked quickly ahead of the Schweitzers, followed by Mr. Christol, and they found themselves back in front of their own house, a small crowd having appeared seemingly out of nowhere.

Dr. Schweitzer considered his options. There was no hospital or even building equipment. The medicines were packed away in boxes waiting to be brought down the river. Though he spoke fluent German, French, and English, he did not speak the local dialects.

"Can you please divide up the people? Those who speak French on this side of the porch. The others, over on that side." The boy happily complied.

Approaching those whom he knew could understand him, Dr. Schweitzer explained the situation: "Good morning. I am sorry to inform you that I do not yet have the medicines to treat any of you at this time. They will be shipped to the island with the next riverboat arriving from Port Gentil. As soon as they arrive, I will be happy to treat you." He stopped, and a small smile appeared on his face. "A doctor without his medicine is like a fetishman without his charms."

"We will wait to hear the sound of the ship's siren," a French-speaking local replied, as the others nodded in agreement.

Dr. Schweitzer, encouraged by the positive response, continued: "I need help to build the hospital. It is imperative that those who are sick have a safe and clean place to recover. During the next three weeks, only those who are able to work should come here to aid in this project. If you come here, you must be able and willing to work, after which time, I will be more than happy to see all who come."

Schweitzer asked the boy if he thought it necessary to translate the message to those who did not speak French.

"I think they all understood enough of it," the boy replied.

The crowd dispersed, many returning to their pirogues and heading up or down the river. Before long, drums sounded, relaying his message, or some form of it, to distant villages: "Oganga—the white fetishman—has come among us. He is powerless until his charms arrive with the next boat."

Fetishes were charms that the local witch doctors used in chasing away evil spirits. All medicine men were considered fetishmen. Sickness—in the minds of Africans at that time—was caused either by evil spirits that entered a body to cause mischief or by another person's magic. Another common belief was that a worm traveled through a body, creating disease or sickness in the stomach or head.[1] That diseases were caused through natural means was not a consideration.

By that time, Ellenberger had arrived and watched the exchange.

"You handled that splendidly," Mr. Christol assured the doctor.

"Thank you. But I had been informed that a local man, named N'Zeng, would assist me as an interpreter."

"We will ensure that one of the canoes will pass the message on to N'Zeng's village that you have arrived and are in need of his assistance."

Schweitzer nodded his appreciation.

"There is something you must know, Doctor," he continued. "If you are to remain here any length of time. These natives will let you down every time. You cannot depend on them."[2]

Schweitzer had never been one to pass judgment. He knew there were many thoughts on what was best for "the natives," by people of the nations that had begun colonies throughout Africa. There were many, though, who did not care about what was best for the African people. Only what was best for business.

"I appreciate your input, Mr. Ellenberger." He paused to take a breath and wipe the sweat from his brow. "Yet I have faced more disappointment than N'Zeng's lack of punctuality. What about the hospital I expected upon my arrival? Or at least the building material? I was informed that these things were to be taken care of."

"We know nothing of those things," Mr. Ellenberger responded, and Mr. Christol nodded his assent. "You will have to wait until our next mission meeting, in July, to ask the administrators."

"That I will do."

Dr. Schweitzer had prepared for years, learning of medicines and treatment, studying the human physique and a myriad of ailments. After receiving his medical degree, he took a special course in tropical diseases and their treatments in order to better understand the needs of the African people. He had not realized, however, that a great portion of his time would have to be devoted to administration, planning, and even common labor.

"I doubt that people will be able to wait until the completion of a hospital building, especially when the location has not even been determined. Is there no place I can use in the meantime? Perhaps one of the schoolrooms?"

The teachers shook their heads. "We are already overcrowded. There is no space," said Mr. Ellenberger.

"Unless, of course, you want to use the old chicken coop," Mr. Christol said, attempting to lighten the tone of the conversation. Upon considering all options, Schweitzer realized the unused coop might have to do for now. He took up a shovel and scrub brush and immediately went to work. The walls were enclosed and whitewashed, the roof repaired, and by the time the siren announced the arrival of his medical supplies from Port Gentil three weeks later, the makeshift hospital room was ready. Until that point, Dr. Schweitzer had been treating a few patients each day, but all the preparatory work kept treatments to a minimum.

The seventy boxes of medicine and equipment were brought downstream in canoes from the riverbank to the mission of Lambaréné. The remainder of the day was spent laboriously carrying the boxes up the hill to the Schweitzers' small home and then carefully unpacking and checking the contents, ensuring they weren't damaged from the long voyage.

The following morning, Dr. Schweitzer stepped out of his house to see that a crowd had formed once more. His heart was touched by all the pain and sadness on the faces waiting for him.

Most who arrived for treatment were accompanied by a family member. The distress on the faces of those suffering was reflected in the eyes of their helpers. Uncertainty. Concern. Fear. And yet, there was also hope. Dr. Schweitzer realized— with a twinge of apprehension and a surge of optimism—that their hope rested in his medical abilities. A strong sense of responsibility for the suffering people came over him. *Is this what it means to be "moved with compassion"?* he mused, reflecting on how often the phrase was used in the gospels.

Hélène stood behind Albert. "There are enough to fill a hospital," she whispered.

"And all we have is a verandah. Well, we cannot wait any longer. We must begin treatment."

Thus their practice began, with Dr. Schweitzer seeing patients on the front verandah, and Mrs. Schweitzer handing him supplies from inside the screened door. They were occupied all morning until a sudden downpour washed through the village right before lunch. It ended just as suddenly, but not before Dr. Schweitzer realized he would need to use the coop as a temporary hospital. It would have to do, for now. He just hoped no one would need any major surgery until the hospital was built. Although it had been cleaned and repaired, he couldn't imagine operating on someone in an old chicken coop.

=====

One of Dr. Schweitzer's first patients, a young man named Joseph Azoawani, from the Galoa tribe, offered to stay on at the mission. He was Schweitzer's first assistant and served as interpreter as well. Having worked as a cook for Europeans, he was fluent in French, and Dr. Schweitzer found his assistance helpful in many ways. His familiarity with cooking terminology caused confusion at times: "This man's right leg of mutton hurts him," or "This woman has a pain in her upper left cutlet."[3]

Not long after that, N'Zeng, the assistant whom Dr. Schweitzer originally expected, also arrived. N'Zeng was a Pahouin; Joseph was a Galoa. Dr. Schweitzer chose to keep both as assistants, each one able to effectively communicate with the members of their tribe who received treatment at the hospital.

Each morning they read out half a dozen rules, each in his own dialect as well as in French:

The Doctor's Standing Orders

1. Spitting near the doctor's house is strictly forbidden.
2. Those who are waiting must not talk to each other loudly.

3. Patients and their friends must bring with them food enough for one day, as they cannot all be treated early in the day.

4. Anyone who spends the night on the station without the doctor's permission will be sent away without any medicine. [Patients sometimes entered the schoolboys' sleeping quarters and took their beds, leaving the boys nowhere to sleep.]

5. All bottles and tin boxes in which medicines are given must be returned.

6. In the middle of the month, when the steamer has gone up the river, none but urgent cases can be seen till the steamer has gone down again, as the doctor is then writing to Europe to get more of his valuable medicines.[4]

The days passed quickly, turning into weeks, which flowed into months. Patients needed constant attention and care, and it was not easy to operate between their house and the coop. Dr. Schweitzer knew that once the dry season began in May, they would need to focus on building a real hospital building as quickly as possible before the rains began in September.

Yet the satisfaction of seeing people revived, their pain diminished, filled Schweitzer's heart. It had not been an easy task to ignore the many objections and arguments from his friends and family or to venture deep into the primeval forests of Africa, but "just to see the joy of those who are plagued with sores, when these have been cleanly bandaged up and they no longer have to drag their poor, bleeding feet through the mud, makes it worth while."[5]

          =====

At the end of July, Dr. Schweitzer rose early one morning long before the break of day. He made his way down to the bank and stepped into a long pirogue, where Mr. Ellenberger and Mr. Christol were waiting, along with a dozen boatmen. He took his place sitting in a folding chair near the bow, their goods behind them in the middle of the canoe—mattresses, tin boxes, and bunches of bananas for the natives to eat during the journey. They were heading thirty-five miles upstream to Samkita for the missionary conference. It was Dr. Schweitzer's first long journey by canoe.

They pushed off, and the natives began their song, which boatmen used to keep in time with each other. The song began with verses referring humorously to the necessity of waking so early that morning. Dawn's first light broke through the sky as they entered a main section of the Ogowe River, revealing dark outlines moving in the water ahead. The singing stopped. The boatmen swiftly moved toward the middle of the stream to make a wide berth around the figures. It was Schweitzer's first view of hippopotami. He had heard of the damage that they could do to boats. It was too common for a hippo to dive underwater and break the surface right under a canoe, smashing it into pieces and sending its owners swimming for dear life to escape its vicious teeth. This particular trip carried no such peril, much to the relief of the fifteen men in the wooden canoe.

As they traveled upstream, Schweitzer knew he would never grow weary of the foliage on either side of him. It was difficult to determine where the river ended and land began. Immense roots grew into the water, clothed with colorfully flowered creepers. The straight, slender trunks of palm trees rose out of the water near the banks. Beyond them, clustered families of palms grew, interspersed by the gnarled trunks of ordinary trees, branches spread broadly, sunlight shafting through the spaces between the wide green leaves. Occasionally, the deep green needles of a pine tree rose high past the canopy of leaves.

As the sun rose, its shimmering reflection burned the travelers' skin. Dr. Schweitzer wiped the sweat from his face and straightened the pith helmet. It might have been hot, but he knew he couldn't risk removing the hat, even for a short time. The sun's rays were too strong. Even half an hour's exposure to the late-afternoon sun of West Gabon, only thirty miles from the equator, was known to cause high fever and delirium or sunstroke.

"Watch out for those flies," Mr. Christol spoke up, shooing a tiny creature away from his dark yellow clothing.

Schweitzer had noticed the flies, about half the size of the housefly he was accustomed to in Europe. "The tsetse. Amazing how something so small can cause such a devastating disease as the sleeping sickness. I don't think a single one has landed on me yet. Perhaps they are fonder of you, Mr. Christol."

"No, watch how they swarm about the natives as well," Mr. Ellenberger observed. "It's the color. You and I are wearing white, Doctor. These flies are smart. They won't land where they can easily be seen and swatted."

"It might be wise to wear white upon our return trip, Mr. Christol."

He answered his colleagues with an exasperated smile as he shooed yet another pest from his clothing, knowing that the bite of the fly was easily able to pierce through his clothing and into his flesh.

At midday, the men directed the pirogue into the shallows and onto a landing near a small village. The dozen boatmen took their only provisions—bananas—and roasted them while Dr. Schweitzer and the two teachers enjoyed pineapples—quenching their thirst with the sweet tangy juice.

They arrived at their destination in the late evening and remained in Samkita for one week. Dr. Schweitzer was pleased with the responses to his requests. The original plan had been for the hospital buildings to be constructed in a more remote area of the mission grounds, but now he would be able to erect them closer to his house. He also had funds to work with; the mission gave him four thousand francs toward building costs.

The next challenge was finding laborers willing to clear the land. It was a small miracle when a timber merchant came through the mission and agreed to let Dr. Schweitzer use eight of his strong workmen. Within two days, the land was level and ready for the building to commence. Schweitzer had already made rough sketches as the ideas formed in his head of the best way to build the hospital.

He realized that the dynamics of an entirely different

culture and background would not allow him to build the hospital in his original design. Between thirty and forty sick or injured people arrived on a daily basis. Sometimes they were dropped off at the landing. More often than not, family members accompanied the patients. These helpers remained with the patients during their entire period of recovery, needing a place to stay and usually food to eat.

———

One morning in mid-August, a man in severe pain was helped into the consulting area. His face was contorted in agony. An examination quickly revealed to the doctor that he had a strangulated hernia. The doctor did not need to be convinced that surgery was necessary in order to save the man's life.

"I will need to operate right away," Dr. Schweitzer informed his wife. "It is a pity the new building is not yet complete."

Mrs. Schweitzer rushed from the old chicken coop and ran to Mr. Christol's schoolroom. The students had gone for lunch, and the room was empty. Upon hearing about the situation, Mr. Christol quickly volunteered the use of his schoolroom.

"The students can have the afternoon off. I will have it cleaned with antiseptics."

"Thank you. We will return soon with the patient."

Dr. Schweitzer readied the instruments while Mrs. Schweitzer prepared the anesthesia. The patient was taken to the schoolroom, and Albert Schweitzer conducted his first major surgery in Africa.

It was a successful one.

Dr. Schweitzer observed that hernias were quite common in Lambaréné, more so than in Europe. He realized with a mixture of emotion that if no doctor is in the vicinity, those suffering from strangulated hernias would end up suffering a painful death, from which a timely operation could have rescued them.

The people faced a variety of ailments more serious than Dr. Schweitzer anticipated. Some of the diseases he treated during his first months in Lambaréné were leprosy, skin diseases, malaria, heart complaints, dysentery, ulcers, urinary issues, and the dreaded sleeping sickness.

Upon departure, each patient was given a circular piece of cardboard hanging from a string. A unique number was written on each cardboard piece, which corresponded with its number on the register where information about the patient was written—the ailment, treatment given, and other pertinent information. At first, Dr. Schweitzer assumed these items would be lost upon a patient's return—as medicine bottles and many other items loaned out never seemed to make their way back to the hospital. However, the numbered cardboard was seldom lost or misplaced; the patients considered it a sort of fetish and wore it at all times.

Fetishes often were comprised of items kept in a small bag, a box, or a buffalo horn. The items included small amounts of earth, red feathers, leopards' claws or teeth, bells from Europe (which became popular as trade grew in the eighteenth century), and usually a piece of human skull—which needed to be provided by someone killed for the specific purpose of providing the fetish. Fetishes were thought to have the power to bring good luck and success to the holder or bad luck, sickness, or death to those whom the holder wished to harm.

———

Mrs. Schweitzer found her niche in preparing for and assisting her husband during operations and monitoring the recovery of more severe cases. She also kept the instruments sterilized and in good condition, dressed the patients' bandages, and ensured the linen was clean. All her duties in the hospital were in addition to the many aspects of housekeeping in the African environment, which took more time than she was accustomed to. Yet she worked valiantly and wholeheartedly.

At the beginning of their medical practice, Hélène also prepared food for the patients and their attendants, yet Dr. Schweitzer noticed that they would not eat the food.

"Joseph," he asked his orderly one day, "I noticed something strange. The patients are not eating the meals that my wife prepares, even though she makes them in the local style."

"Doctor, you cannot expect them to eat food that has been prepared by a stranger. My people are very suspicious. Poisoning is a common source of sickness here."

Joseph's reply surprised Schweitzer. "But surely they can't believe that we would attempt to poison them? We have come only to help."

"Not you or the madam, but no one knows who might be passing by, who might stop in the kitchen and touch the ladle with which she is cooking. Even those acts are believed to cause poisoning and sickness."

Dr. Schweitzer was dumbfounded. "Just passing by cannot . . ." He stopped and sighed, realizing the futility of trying to argue the cause of reason when it stood against deeply held beliefs. "Joseph, the patients must eat, or they will not recover. What do you suggest?"

"Let their families prepare the food. Then there will be no fear of unwanted people near the place where the meals are made ready."

Schweitzer recognized the wisdom of Joseph's suggestion, and the announcement was made that evening: a member of every patient's family would be responsible to secure provisions as well as prepare and cook for the patient and himself or herself. The Schweitzers' task was to issue the food supplies each morning to the attendants, who lined up outside the storehouse. Joseph's assistance again proved to be reliable. He brought a great deal of insight into the care of his people at the hospital. He understood their fears, expectations, and thoughts. He spoke ten languages—French and English as well as eight local dialects. Although he could not read or write, he memorized the look of words on medicine bottles and never made a mistake when fetching medicine for the doctor.

―――

In November 1913, seven months after the Schweitzers' arrival, the new hospital building was complete and ready for patients. It was a four-room building; the larger two rooms were thirteen feet square—the outer room for consulting and the inner room for operations. Two small side rooms served as the dispensary and the sterilizing room. The floor was made of cement, and the building itself was constructed of corrugated iron. Its large windows reaching up to the ceiling allowed the hot air to escape. No glass covered the windows, but a wire-mesh netting kept the mosquitoes out. Wide shelves along the walls made use of every corner of the building.

As soon as the first building was complete, work began on the next couple of buildings—a waiting room and a ward for patients. Yet finding laborers often posed a challenge. The flourishing timber trade kept workmen occupied at timber camps for months at a time. Schweitzer located a few day laborers and laid out the project for them. Every evening, he checked on the progress but found that no work whatsoever had been done. A few days into this cycle, he grew impatient with what he perceived to be laziness.

"Doctor, don't shout at us so! It is your own fault. Stay here and we shall work, but if you are in the hospital with the sick folk, we are alone and do nothing,"[6] one man candidly explained their point of view. They would work only under the circumstances that required it.

From that time onward, Dr. Schweitzer ensured that, if he needed to hire day laborers, he was available for at least a few hours of every day to keep the men working. He found this to be a useful solution.

Both buildings were constructed of solid logs interlaid with raffia leaves. The patients' ward was built more than twice as long as it was wide, and inside were two long rows with an aisle down the middle, eight beds on each side. The patients and their attendants moved immediately from the boathouse in which they had been staying. The patients were placed in the hut as the attendants went out, after having been provided with axes and directions, and built the beds—four short posts forked at the tops, that had two long side poles tied to them. Shorter poles of wood were then laid across the longer poles and tied together with stalks. The mattresses were simple—dried grass. The twenty inches left under each bed served as a storage place for cooking utensils, bananas, and personal possessions of the patient and attendant—who sometimes slept next to the patient or on the floor below.

———

One day, a desperately ill man was deposited on the river landing, dropped off on the dirt without even a family member to care for him.

"Joseph, please call some men who can help take this man into the hospital."

"Doctor, turn him away. Call the boatmen back to take him home to his village." Joseph was adamant.

Schweitzer stated firmly: "We do not refuse aid to anyone who needs our help. Please help me carry him to the hospital. Time is wasting."

Joseph obliged without another word, yet he waited nervously outside while Dr. Schweitzer examined the man.

"Please call Mrs. Schweitzer to prepare the instruments

for surgery." Dr. Schweitzer emerged from the consulting room, his face grim.

"Doctor, please do not operate on him." Joseph spoke quietly, but pleadingly.

"Joseph," Schweitzer's voice was stern, "I do not understand your hesitation. If we do not operate, he will die."

"He was turned away by the fetishmen of his tribe. He is beyond hope. If you operate and he dies, his tribe will place the blame on you, although they know that he will die anyway."

Dr. Schweitzer finally understood the reason for his aide's hesitancy. "He might die, yes. Others to come might also die. Medicine is not a perfect practice. There is no one remedy to heal every case, yet much can still be done to ease the pain of those suffering. I will do whatever I can until I can do no more."

"I understand. I will fetch the madam," Joseph replied, complying with the doctor's wishes.

Dr. Schweitzer tried to ignore the feelings of trepidation as he worked deftly on the ailing man. He knew there would be more who would come to him, those who had no hope except what he could offer. But was it enough? If the operation was a success, people would consider that he was capable of performing the miraculous. If it failed, the stronghold of the fetishmen and witch doctors with their charms and medicines would take an even stronger hold in the surrounding villages. He said a silent prayer as he continued his procedure.

Schweitzer's skill and dedication were rewarded. The man survived the procedure. As he slowly came out of the effects of the anesthesia, his eyes began to focus. He then reached out and grabbed Dr. Schweitzer's hand. "The pain! The pain is gone!" Schweitzer smiled and held the hand tightly.

All of the doctor's early operations were a success. Sometimes afterward, he explained to his helpers and the attendants what had brought him to Africa as a doctor—the example of Jesus, who reached out to the needy and healed the sick. As they sat side by side, Dr. Schweitzer was filled with the joy and truth of the words: "All ye are brethren" (Matt. 23:8).[7]

═══

During their first year, in spite of a steady stream of sick and afflicted people, Dr. and Mrs. Schweitzer maintained good health. They felt this a blessing because they had many to care for on a daily basis, among the multitude of other duties.

In early 1914, Schweitzer began a time-consuming and expensive building project—erecting a hut for victims of sleeping sickness. Sleeping sickness (*trypanosomiasis*) had existed for quite some time, yet the travel boundaries kept epidemics at bay. However, when European traders traveled to equatorial Africa, they took on local people as crew and servants. In cases where the locals were carriers of sleeping sickness, they spread it from one location to the next and the next. Thirty years before Albert Schweitzer arrived in Africa, sleeping sickness was unheard of along the Ogowe River, but in recent decades it devastated village after village, becoming a common and dreaded disease in West Africa.

A decade before Albert Schweitzer journeyed to Africa, English doctors discovered the cause of sleeping sickness:

a flagellate (organism with a propulsive tail) they called *Trypanosoma brucei*. The tsetse fly acts as carrier of the parasite, which—once it enters the bloodstream through a bite—begins to reproduce.

Early symptoms included irregular fevers and headaches, which were often misdiagnosed until the more severe symptoms of rheumatism and constant fatigue appeared. A sufferer felt the need to sleep all of the time. Eventually, as the parasites entered the nervous system, symptoms increased, bringing dementia and convulsions. The victim then fell into a coma from which he often never awakened. Bedsores developed, and the stricken individual often succumbed to death after contracting pneumonia or another common ailment. Even with modern medicine, sleeping sickness must be discovered in its early stages before the parasites enter the central nervous system, or it is fatal.

For Dr. Schweitzer, it was a complicated affair to determine such an elusive diagnosis. A microscopic evaluation of the blood was necessary to determine whether parasites existed in the bloodstream, yet the parasite might be seen only in one out of five samples. Diagnosing just two such patients kept the doctor at his microscope all morning, unavailable to treat the number of ailing people waiting outside. Other patients, recovering from surgeries, required cleansing and fresh bandages; a constant flow of people needing medicines also took valuable time. It was clear that there was more work than one doctor and nurse could effectively manage.

One evening, Dr. Schweitzer's mood was melancholy after a long and trying day. He stepped outside into the evening air, trying to enjoy the lively symphony of the forest creatures and insects. But he felt that something was missing.

His wife noticed his face was tensely set. "Is everything all right?"

"They all seem able to make their own music. They are at home. I have not played the piano once since arriving." Organ playing was one great passion of the doctor, which he assumed he would be required to sacrifice upon his decision to move to Africa.

"I noticed. You were given such a lovely piano by the Paris Bach Society. They so appreciated all you did during your time with them."

"Yes, they even lined it with zinc to survive the tropical weather."

"So why don't you play?"

Albert smiled grimly. "I don't have the heart. I think it would be easier in a way not to play. Just let my fingers and feet grow rusty from lack of use. I'm in Africa now; I'm serving the people as a doctor, no longer a musician."

"Yes, you are a doctor, following the example of Christ to heal. But that does not mean you have to let go of everything in which you find enjoyment."

Her words settled in his heart, and when he stepped into their small house on the edge of the forest, he sat down at the piano. Within a few moments, a new melody mingled with the chorus of the evening and brought smiles to many careworn faces at the hospital compound.

From that time on, Schweitzer spent many evenings practicing Bach, Mendelssohn, Widor, and other composers, even if he had only a half hour to spare between his other duties.

The doctor also found great joy in other things besides medicine, especially preaching. He preached at the Church of St. Nicholas in Strasbourg for nearly fifteen years, and it brought him deep satisfaction to be allowed to share with the congregation the messages of God's love and Jesus' example to mankind. It was only natural that he relished sharing that same message with his African congregation. He spoke simply, one sentence at a time, which was then interpreted into the local dialects: "And it seemed to him a glorious thing to preach about Jesus and Paul to people unfamiliar with them."[8]

4

The Peaceful Prisoner of War

We must realize that all life is valuable and that we are
united to all life. From this knowledge comes our spiritual
relationship with the universe.

—ALBERT SCHWEITZER

1914–18

During August of 1914, Albert and Hélène Schweitzer were in the middle of an expected dry season. They were also in the middle of a war. Although World War I began at the end of July, news didn't reach Lambaréné until the fifth of August.

The Schweitzers had returned from Cape Lopez only three days before. There they had stayed at the home of a man whose wife had been treated by Dr. Schweitzer. This time, it was Schweitzer recovering from a painful abscess in his foot. By the time they arrived at the practice of the military doctor in Cape Lopez, the abscess had burst on its own. Now the doctor and his wife had nothing to do but breathe in the invigorating sea breeze for a few days on the bay. From his vantage point in an armchair on the verandah, the doctor had the opportunity to write on the topic of the raftsmen and lumbermen who traveled along the Ogowe River.

Schweitzer often glanced up from his writing to take in the sight of gentle waves flowing through the sand or the breeze teasing the palm fronds, which whispered their response to the wind.

The two-hundred-mile journey from Cape Lopez back to

Lambaréné took three days on board a cargo steamer. During that trip, Schweitzer utilized his time once more in writing, this time on social problems in the forests of Gabon.

Upon their return, Dr. and Mrs. Schweitzer went back to work immediately. The backlog of responsibilities was overwhelming.

"Joseph, I have just mixed this medication for a woman who is ill in Cape Lopez. Can you please ask the supply store if they will convey it to her via the steamer's next journey north?"

"Yes, Doctor."

With that, Joseph was off. He returned with an unexpected reply from the supply store owner: "In Europe they are mobilizing and probably already at war. We must place our steamer at the disposal of the authorities and cannot say when it will go next to Cape Lopez."

The Schweitzers had only a few hours to adjust to the news—and almost no time to determine what it might mean for them—before they found themselves in a difficult position. Albert Schweitzer had grown up in Alsace—a small province claimed by both Germany and France. He was now living in Gabon, a colony of French Equatorial Africa. Directly north of Gabon rested Cameroon—governed by Germany. The war between France and Germany was not only raging in Europe, but reaching as far as the borders of their hospital. That very evening, the Schweitzers became prisoners of war by the Germans. With local people stationed outside their home as guards, they were confined to house arrest under the strict order that Dr. Schweitzer was forbidden to see or treat anyone.

The Schweitzers had been planning a furlough in Europe as an extended period of recuperation. What would happen to these plans? And the patients? Schweitzer refused to give in to discouragement and despair. He chose to turn this time of confinement into an opportunity. On the second morning, he woke up early and stepped into the outer room. He sat at his writing desk, the light morning breeze whispering through the open door. Moving aside various stacks of loose papers, he began to write, his mind in labor to give birth to a thought that had been conceived more than fifteen years earlier.

In summer 1899, Schweitzer had just earned his doctorate in philosophy from the University of Strasbourg. That summer, Albert stayed with friends in Berlin. He was impressed by the intellectuals of that city as well as by their simple way of life, and he found it was easier to adjust there than to the widely diverse city of Paris. He and a small group of students were conversing together one evening when the subject of a recent class at the university arose. One of his friends remarked, "We are all of us just nothing but [children]!"[1]

The words struck a chord within Schweitzer: *Why, that is just what I have felt as well. Mankind has made great strides of progress in the sphere of inventions. Knowledge has grown as never before. We assume that this growth has automatically spread into the areas of ethics and philosophy, but it has not. In fact, from what I have perceived, our intellectual condition—and even our spiritual state—is declining from that of generations past. We are living on their accomplishments and have stopped striving to make further progress.*[2]

From that evening in the home of a university professor,

a book began to develop in Schweitzer's mind. The working title was *We Inheritors of a Past*.[3] Portions of the book, like so many pieces of a puzzle, lay scattered among the recesses of his mind for years. But now those pieces were coming together. As people around the world faced the scourge of war, the reality of a fallen civilization was all about them. *If the catastrophe has already come about, what good is deliberation about the causes, which are now apparent to everyone?*[4] The question haunted him.

Through the hidden blessing of being forbidden to treat patients, Dr. Schweitzer now had time to sit and write. And write he did—yet with the uncertainty of being detained as a prisoner of war far from his home country. *What will become of this work?* he wondered. *Will I ever return home?*

By November, Dr. Schweitzer was granted permission to resume his practice in Lambaréné and the surrounding villages. He returned to work with renewed vigor at the opportunity once more to treat the sick and diseased and to care for the needy.

One busy morning, Dr. Schweitzer and his assistant, Joseph, were dressing the wounds of patients when Joseph let out his pent-up frustration.

"The prices in Lambaréné have gone up *again*. Everything is far above the price it was a few months ago. These Europeans! They need to solve their problems and end the war so that things can be affordable once more."

"Joseph," Dr. Schweitzer cut him short. "You must realize that higher prices are only a small effect of the war. Have you not noticed the worried expressions that we 'foreigners' are bearing these days? Our countrymen are dying, and we pray for them each day that the war will end for the sake of those whose lives are in danger on the front lines."[5]

Joseph looked into the face of the doctor in surprise, a realization dawning on him of the true cost of war.

"Yet how can it be, Doctor? Your people have brought to this nation the message of God's love, of Christ and his compassion and mercy. But now they are killing each other. They are not following the instructions of Jesus Christ."

A wave of sadness washed over Schweitzer. How many others throughout the nation of Africa were asking this same question? How many who had received the message of Christ were now disillusioned, unable to reconcile the contradiction in their minds? How many whose lives were illuminated by the light of Jesus' love now grew confused by the spreading darkness of war?

"I cannot explain it. We stand before something terrible, something incomprehensible.[6] Yet as long as there are those who continue to manifest mercy, kindness, and the love of Christ, hope will remain."

"And this is why you have come?"

"My heart is consoled by the fact that, when so much wrong is being done in this world, I can still do good and help others."

———

December 1914. Christmas. The world still pitched and swayed from the winds of war, and the Schweitzers remained far from home and loved ones. They placed candles on a small palm tree. Watching the gentle glow slowly melt through the candles, Schweitzer recalled the words, "Ye are the light of the world. . . . Neither do men light a candle, and put it under a bushel, but on a candlestick; and it giveth light unto all that are in the house" (Matt. 5:14–15). Perhaps their light was small, but they would keep the faint light burning.

When the candles had dwindled in size to half their original height, he blew out the flames. "What are you doing?" his wife asked.

"They are all we have," Albert replied candidly, "and we must keep them for next year."

"Next year?" Hélène sighed and shook her head.[7] *Another year?*

The villagers of Lambaréné and its surrounding regions had begun feeling the fuller effects of the war. Initially, the only issue was the increase in prices.

Now, the economy began to plummet as one logging camp after another closed down because shipments of lumber were no longer possible. The rapid growth of industry and cultural development halted without warning as missionaries and teachers were called back to their home countries. The mode of living in Africa had been changing over the previous hundred years, and now there was no way to go back to the preindustrial age, yet few remained to help move the nation forward.[8]

Dr. Schweitzer often checked the medical supplies, grateful that cases of drugs had arrived on the last ship that arrived from Europe before the war began. *How long will they last?*

he wondered. *How long will we have what we need to keep the hospital running?*

Food was another concern. The doctor instructed patients to bring their own supply of bananas. He did his best to provide patients with rice when they used up their meager supplies. Toward the end of 1915, Schweitzer knew he would have to further ration supplies because there was no guarantee when they would again be available.

In September 1915, Dr. Schweitzer traveled to the mission base of N'Gomo to treat Madame Pelot, a missionary's wife who had been ill. This trip would forever stand out in his mind as the time that his life's philosophy came together in a simple, resounding phrase. As he made the slow journey upstream aboard an overloaded steamer, he struggled to resolve the missing element in his philosophy. Albert scribbled a sentence here, a paragraph there, trying to connect his thoughts to form a clear, foundational ethical concept. Finally, at a time he least expected it, it happened:

> On the third day, at the very moment when, at sunset, we were making our way through a herd of hippopotamuses, there flashed upon my mind, unforeseen and unsought, the phrase, "Reverence for Life." The iron door had yielded: the path in the thicket had become visible. Now I had found my way to the idea in which world- and life-affirmation and ethics are contained side by side! Now I knew that the world-view of ethical world- and life-affirmation, together with its ideals of civilization, is founded in thought.[9]

Reverence for life.

The philosophy originated from the concept that each man carries within himself a deep will-to-live, which must be recognized not only in oneself, but also in all of mankind and extended to the animal kingdom. Man naturally affirms, through reverence for life and respect of all living forms, his will-to-live and that of others. The "thinking" man is aware of his responsibility to respect all forms of life. Even though he is, time and again, required to sacrifice some forms of life in order to continue living, he is ever conscious of the will-to-live present within every life. He reveres life of every form for its mysterious attributes that can come only from God:

> The Reverence for Life . . . aim[s] to create values, and to realize progress of different kinds which shall serve the material, spiritual, and ethical development of men and mankind. While the unthinking modern world- and life-affirmation stumbles about with its ideals of power won by discovery and invention, the thinking world- and life-affirmation sets up the spiritual and ethical perfecting of mankind as the highest ideal, and an ideal from which alone all other ideals of progress get their real value.[10]

Albert Schweitzer delved into these concepts. He pondered and prayed, measured and mused, weighed and wrote. Two volumes resulted: *The Decay and Restoration of Civilization* and *Civilization and Ethics*.[11]

Their second war Christmas saw the last flame of the

candles dwindle and fade on the Christmas palm tree, presaging challenging times.

Heavy rains during the end of the year threatened the hospital building. Albert knew he must take advantage of the dry season, which would last only a couple of months, to lay stone gutters in strategic places around the hospital. The waters that flowed down the hill toward the building during the rainy season would be diverted around it. Next, a wall was needed around the largest hospital ward to protect it fully from the devastating effects of the frequent rainstorms. The project took up every spare moment over a four-month period, Dr. Schweitzer often having to pitch in with the manual labor to instruct his laborers and to keep them from walking off the job.[12]

Upon completion of the construction projects, Albert unearthed a tiny army of termites that had discovered his cases of bandages and drugs. It took weeks to unpack, clean out, and repack every item from the affected cases. The guilty item was finally discovered: a loose lid on a bottle of medicinal syrup.[13] Schweitzer was beginning to understand that nature would serve as a continual combat zone in the battle to keep the hospital in good working condition.

———

Albert completed his accounting and looked up, gazing upon nothing in particular. He sighed. Since the war began, no funds had arrived from Strasbourg. He had cut as many corners as possible, yet still the debts mounted.

"Joseph, would you please see me after the work period has ended?"

"Certainly, Dr. Schweitzer."

The inevitable could be postponed no longer.

"You wished to speak with me?"

"Joseph, you know how much I have valued your work over these years, especially in recent months."

"Yes. Things have been difficult."

"With my funding having been cut off as a result of the war, I am incurring debts. As such, I must reconsider expenses. Would you be willing to continue work at this hospital for 50 percent of your wages until circumstances improve?"

"Dr. Schweitzer, that would be only thirty-five francs."

"I would not ask it of you except that finances have now become a matter of extreme concern. I am only acting out of necessity so that the hospital may continue to run."

"I am sorry. I cannot continue working for such low wages." Joseph squared his shoulders. "My dignity would not allow me to serve you for so small a sum."

"Then I regret to hear of your decision. I suppose, though, that you must act on your own convictions and that of your dignity."

From that point onward, Dr. Schweitzer's workload increased drastically as he assumed many responsibilities previously undertaken by his assistant. Another assistant, N'Kendju, worked at the hospital, yet his accomplishments on any given day rested on his somewhat undependable moods.

By now Schweitzer and his wife suffered from anemia due to a poor diet and constant fatigue brought on by their taxing circumstances. However, the doctor was relieved to find that in spite of his poor physical health, he remained alert mentally. In the evenings, if he was not too tired, he sat at his table deep into the night. Enjoying the occasional breeze that sauntered through the lattice door, with the chorus of the toads and the crickets to accompany his thoughts, Albert continued his study of the philosophy of civilization and ethics. With a dwarf antelope resting at his feet, and his dog, Caramba, faithfully keeping watch out on the verandah, Schweitzer enjoyed the solitude and let it guide his thoughts as he wrote.

A small number of foreigners, those who had not been able to return home with the onset of the war, had begun to show signs of exhaustion. In groups of two and three, they traveled to the hospital "for repairs," as they called it.[14] Dr. Schweitzer donated the use of his personal room to these patients and relocated to the front verandah, which had been enclosed with screens to keep mosquitoes away. If patients argued that the doctor should remain in his own room, he brushed them away by saying: "There's more fresh air on the verandah."

The precious stock of condensed milk was a great benefit to the health of the recovering foreigners, as was the special diet that Hélène provided for them each day. She worked wonders with what was available to create a healthy menu for the invalids—even if all the protein available was monkey meat.

By the end of 1916, the Schweitzers also found it necessary to recuperate, mainly for Hélène's sake. They traveled to Chienga, near Cape Lopez, to spend the rainy season by the coast, where a timber merchant had given them use of an empty house that overlooked a branch of the Ogowe River.[15]

Albert Schweitzer soon found himself busy once more, having volunteered to aid the timber merchant by joining his team of laborers. They worked through the high tides to roll logs from the river onto dry land. The logs had been tied together in rafts for the journey from the timber site to the mouth of the Ogowe. Here they remained, a looming and forlorn reminder that shipping between Europe and Africa had ceased during the war. The greatest threat for the logs was the bore worm, which could easily destroy an entire shipment, so the greatest need was to roll the timber to a dry area. Each log weighed between two and three tons, and it often took hours to hoist, pull, and move just one of them.

During low tide, eager patients visited Schweitzer. Although a doctor practiced at Cape Lopez, many preferred Schweitzer's services. Every spare moment Schweitzer continued to write, and now his work was *The Philosophy of Civilization*.

======

Albert and Hélène had barely resumed the work at Lambaréné when, in September 1917, they received the order to leave on a ship that was due any day. Their destination: a prison camp in Europe. Although their hearts sank at this turn of events, once again they were powerless against the giant, unfeeling war machine. The ship was delayed a few days, and the remaining missionaries—as well as some of the local people—worked feverishly with the doctor and his wife as they packed their possessions, instruments, medicines, and bandages into cases.

"Will we return, I wonder, to resume our work here one day?" Albert said as he carefully latched the iron door, after having placed their remaining supplies in a small building made of corrugated iron.

"In God's time, we shall see." His wife's words were encouraging, though he knew just how draining these last years had been on her health. Right now the future was darkened by the shadow of the war, and there was no way to know what it might hold.

"Doctor, Doctor, please come quickly!" The call from one of the recuperating patients broke his train of thought.

They hurried to the main hospital ward, where a man in severe pain was waiting, his face contorted in agony. The diagnosis was quickly made—a strangulated hernia. *My first operation here was a strangulated hernia,* Schweitzer thought. *Now it looks like it might be my last.* No time could be wasted. There on the fringe of the priveval forest, the doctor and his wife prepared for one more surgery.

Through his last two nights in Lambaréné, Albert Schweitzer painstakingly copied down an outline of his *Philosophy of Civilization* in French. He made it out to look like an innocent historical document chronicling past ages. He then gave the manuscript in its entirety to an American missionary, Mr. Ford, who had been working in Lambaréné at the time. Schweitzer kept only the French outline.

"I trust that you will be able to keep this safe until such a time as you can return it to me once more."

"I must say, in all honesty, that my preference would be to see this manuscript resting on the bottom of the river." Mr. Ford's response was straightforward, yet not unkind. "I have not been impressed by my experience with the uses of philosophy. I believe it does more harm than good to the cause of Christianity. Yet I will keep it safe, as you have asked, according to the best of my ability."

"My prayer, Mr. Ford, is that one day Christians will unite around the philosophy of reverence for life and find that, in their common goal, they will rebuild the world and usher in the kingdom of God."

With their preparations nearly over, Schweitzer only needed to exchange the gold they had been keeping in case of emergency. The ship had arrived at Lambaréné, and they were to board within an hour. Albert and Hélène quickly made their way to the home of an English timber merchant.

"Do you remember," Albert asked his wife with a smile, "when you asked whether it was necessary to bring this gold all the way to Africa?"

"You told me we might need it in case of war. How far away those days seem now."

"Days of peace will come once more. We must keep faith and hope always."

They exchanged their gold for French banknotes and sewed the notes into the lining of their clothing before heading to the dock, which was swarming with people.

"There are so many! Have they all come to board the ship?" Mrs. Schweitzer asked quietly.

"I don't think so," Albert responded, as everyone in the crowd seemed to be focused solely upon their approach.

Some faces were trying to smile. Others were on the brink of tears. Still others had already begun to cry. As Albert and Hélène trudged heavily toward the gangplank, weighed down by more than the bags they carried, their steps were softened by well wishes, their fears lightened by words of deep gratitude, their hearts warmed by smiles, handshakes, and hugs.

They were already on board when the Father Superior of the Catholic mission at Lambaréné strode up and onto the ship. "You shall not leave this country without my thanking you both for all the good that you have done it."[16] His words were sincere and greatly treasured.

During the short stop at Cape Lopez, another man boarded the ship for a moment. "You treated my wife at your hospital," he said, shaking the doctor's hand. "Please take this as a token of my appreciation." He offered Schweitzer some money before departing as rapidly as he approached.

As the ship left, Albert watched the land fade into the background. What was first distinctly evident as leaves and branches began to merge together until they were one squiggly strand of green stitching together two vast patchworks of blue—the sky and the ocean.

The doctor, who had given his time unceasingly during the past four years, pondered the fate of the African people. *How many will suffer lack of treatment in light of our departure? How many more will be affected by the horrors of war, pressed into service for a conflict they know nothing about?* Now, more than ever, he saw the need of true respect for all people, an empathy and understanding among mankind that every single life on earth is a precious miracle—one to be honored, cherished, and protected. He only hoped that, in spite of—and perhaps through—the devastation of this war, mankind would come to understand and embrace the ethic of love and the philosophy of reverence for life.

=====

Even in the midst of the trying circumstances they faced, moments shone through like shafts of sunlight piercing a canopy of dense clouds.

The first such sunburst occurred during the voyage. Although the Schweitzers were considered prisoners of war, their steward treated them kindly and ensured that their voyage was comfortable. As they neared their temporary destination of Bordeaux, the steward approached the couple.

"Have you noticed," he asked in a somewhat arrogant manner, "that the way in which I treated you during the voyage was with a kindness I generally do not bestow on prisoners?"

Unsure of exactly how to respond, Albert Schweitzer smiled and expressed his appreciation: "We are grateful."

The steward continued, "A few months ago, a Mr. Gaucher, whom you had had for months as a patient in your hospital, traveled home in this ship in one of my cabins. 'Gaillard,' he said to me, 'it may happen that before long you will be taking the Lambaréné doctor to Europe as a prisoner. If he ever does travel on your ship, and should you be able to help him in any way, do so for my sake.' Now you know why I treated you well."[17]

The doctor and his wife were deeply touched, their hearts filled with warmth.

After three weeks at temporary quarters in Bordeaux, they were moved to the Pyrenees, where they stayed in an ancient monastery—the Garaison—which had swelled into a large internment camp. Previous detainees—talented artisans among them—had restored the old building, which in ages past had served as a pilgrimage site for the sick.

Dr. and Mrs. Schweitzer had arrived at the camp only the day before. The sun refused to break through the cold, gray sky as Albert stood in the courtyard, shivering at the drastic change in weather.

"Greetings. You are Dr. Schweitzer, are you not?" A fellow prisoner held out his hand in welcome.

"I am." Dr. Schweitzer shook his hand with a smile.

"I am Mill-engineer Borkeloh, and I am in your debt. If there is any way I can serve you during your time here, I would be honored to do so."

"It is a pleasure to meet you, Mr. Borkeloh, yet how could you be in my debt? We have never met."

"Yes, but not long after the war began, you gave medicines to Richard Classen. Do you remember him?"

"I do. Richard Classen. Yes, he worked in Lambaréné, a timber firm representative."

"He was taken as prisoner of war and sent to a camp in Dahomey. From there, he was sent to France, the same internment camp where I was detained with my wife. She had grown ill, and Mr. Classen revived her with those same medicines. I believe her very life was saved. I am truly indebted to you."

Once more, a candle shone through the darkness of war. The soft light that had radiated from the African jungle where a dedicated doctor practiced was being reflected back on him. He realized once more the unsurpassed joy that came through giving one's life in service to others.

Mr. Borkeloh built for the doctor a table made of old wood. Now Dr. Schweitzer had the opportunity to write and even to practice organ playing, using the table as his manual.[18] Practicing thus, as he did when a child, brought back memories of a time that seemed an age ago.

"Albert Schweitzer is my thorn in the flesh."[19] He recalled the words clearly, spoken by his music teacher, Eugen Münch. From the age of ten, Albert stayed with his uncle and aunt in Mulhausen, Alsace, during the school seasons, and attended the Mulhausen Gymnasium.

His aunt ensured that he played piano every evening, yet this typical young teen did not put forth much effort in practicing the pieces his teacher gave him to learn. Instead, he found great joy in improvisation and playing music by sight.

One day, at the end of another session in which young Albert played half-heartedly—partly because he felt uncomfortable in expressing his deep love and passion for the music in front of his teacher—his instructor was exasperated.

The portly man pulled out a volume of Mendelssohn's music and opened it. His annoyance was apparent. "Really you don't deserve to have such beautiful music given you to play. You'll spoil this for me, just like everything else. If a boy has no feeling, I certainly can't give him any!"[20]

Albert saw it was a piece he had played to himself quite

frequently. He smiled, thinking, *I'll show you whether I have any feeling or not!*[21] He went home and practiced every evening that week. The next week, he played for his teacher from that place deep in his soul where the music had always lain.

The teacher did not say a word, but sat beside him and began to play along. Soon Albert was found worthy to begin practicing Bach's music and was given permission to take lessons on the beautiful resonating organ at St. Stephen's—a dream he had long held in his heart.[22] Albert's father was a wonderful organist, and his mother's father had been both organist and organ builder. The seed was sown deep in Albert's heart, and it had blossomed beautifully.

Now, at a small table made of scraps of wood, Schweitzer practiced his talent once more. He did not know when and where he would have the opportunity to play the organ again, and so he took advantage of these peaceful moments in the old monastery.

Dr. Schweitzer soon became busy with medical duties, for he was granted permission to treat the sick. The governor of the camp allowed him to use a small room for consultation and treatment, as well as to store the instruments and medication that Schweitzer had carried with him from Africa. Many prisoners had also arrived from tropical locations and were grateful for a doctor familiar with tropical diseases. He brought relief to many during the five-month detainment.

Dr. Schweitzer did what he could for the ailing but grieved for those who suffered psychologically. They circled the courtyard time and again, like caged animals, stopping to gaze with longing at the glistening Pyrenees mountain range in the distance. In addition to their pitiful mental states, they suffered the constant cold in unheated rooms; malnutrition threatened the health of many. Worse still were the unspoken fears they harbored. All these prisoners had lived and worked in France or one of its many colonies. After the war, what future would they have? No position. No money. No hope.

Albert found inspiration, though, even in such discouraging circumstances. The internees were a diverse group. Before the war, their vocations had been as varied as their lands of origin. From traveling merchants to Catholic missionaries, hotel managers to artists, businessmen to engineers—it seemed every walk of life was represented within the walls of the monastery. He took full advantage of this opportunity as he learned straight from experienced and educated individuals instead of reading books. He garnered information about many things, from banking to factory building, from architecture to equipment, from cereal cultivation to furnace construction.[23]

The approach of spring had never been so welcome after the harsh winter at Garaison. Dr. and Mrs. Schweitzer were assigned to another camp, one primarily for Alsatians, in St. Rémy of Provence, France. They had made themselves at home and did not wish to be relocated. However, in their new location—another old monastery—both Albert and Hélène were happy to be reacquainted with a number of individuals they knew before the war. Albert was also grateful for the opportunity to preach at the weekly services held at St. Rémy.

However, their health rapidly deteriorated. Fierce gusts of wind blew through the valley of Provence, and severe drafts whipped across the cold stone floors of the monastery.

Recurring bouts of dysentery—which Schweitzer caught during their short internment at Bordeaux—also brought on constant fatigue.

Still, the needs of the sick kept Schweitzer, who had been appointed camp doctor, well occupied.

It was July 1918.

"Albert, have you heard?" Hélène's excitement was apparent as she rushed into the room that her husband used for consultation and treatment.

"Heard what?" He smiled to see the flush on her face. Of late her appearance had been thin and drawn, the light fading from her eyes.

"We will be released soon! A prisoner exchange! I heard them speaking in the garden." She stopped a moment to catch her breath. "Oh, could it be true?"

"I will see the governor at once." No more patients were expected, so Schweitzer closed up the room and hurried over to the governor's quarters.

"I have received a list. It is true." The governor, a mild-mannered gentleman from Marseilles, had resumed work during the war although he had already retired from his post as police commissioner. His jovial nature won him respect among the prisoners, and Dr. Schweitzer knew he appreciated his service as camp doctor. Yet the governor's face seemed tense and grave.

"Is everything all right?" Schweitzer felt a twinge of apprehension.

"Your name is not on the list. Your wife's name is there. She will be able to go home."

Schweitzer was silent for a moment, sorting through his emotions. He also thought of the precious life that his wife was now carrying within her.

"Hélène needs to go home. Her health has not been well. Thank you, governor." He turned to go. "Please," he added in an afterthought, "do not tell my wife about the details of the list."

"Certainly."

At hearing the confirmation from her husband, Mrs. Schweitzer was beside herself with joy. "Imagine, in a week's time we will be back in Günsbach. The baby will be born in your hometown!"

Albert shared in his wife's joy but did not say a word.

A couple of nights later, an announcement sounded through the camp, awakening everyone from sleep.

"Prepare for departure. All prisoners, prepare for departure."

Albert was confused. *All* prisoners? Once more, he made his way to find the governor, who was already in his office, busy at work.

"Governor . . ."

"Yes, yes. All prisoners! I received a new list just an hour ago."

Albert raced back to pack their belongings.

As the sun peered over the high walls, the Schweitzers joined the other prisoners in the courtyard, waiting for the examination of their luggage. Finally all checking was complete. They lined up for departure, when Albert remembered the governor. He hurried back to the office and found the man, looking more aged than ever, sitting despondently amidst stacks of paperwork and boxes.

"Thank you for your kindness, sir." Schweitzer's words were heartfelt.

The governor's eyes glistened as he bid farewell to the doctor: "Please do not forget to write me."

"I will write you," Schweitzer promised as he headed back into the sunlight toward freedom.

5

Three Sacrifices Returned

Never say there is nothing beautiful in the world anymore. There is always something to make you wonder in the shape of a tree, the trembling of a leaf.

—ALBERT SCHWEITZER

1918–24

The journey by train from Tarascon, at the southern tip of France, toward their homeland of Alsace remained a poignant image in Schweitzer's mind. The train wended northeast, passing through Switzerland on its way into southern Germany, before turning west once more and arriving in Strasbourg, the Alsace region of eastern France.

Albert and Hélène feasted their eyes on the lush fields and peaceful houses of the Swiss countryside. To see mile after mile, town after town, untouched by the devastation of war filled their hearts with hope. A welcoming surprise met the Schweitzers at the Zürich station when they were met by a number of friends, relieved at their release and joyful to see them once more. The long train journey continued.

Konstanz, in southwest Germany, bordering Switzerland, stood in stark contrast to the vibrant landscape of Switzerland. They had only heard the stories of starvation, but now they saw for themselves as gaunt figures wandered the war-torn streets. However, in Konstanz, Hélène had a joyful reunion with her parents, and they gained permission to take her to their home in Strasbourg. Albert remained in the city one more day, completing the necessary paperwork.

Upon arrival in Strasbourg, Albert immediately sought permission to find his father. Although Günsbach was only fifty-five miles from Strasbourg, it was near military grounds and required special permission from the German authorities. Finally he was able to secure passage by train as far as Colmar and then had to travel the final ten miles by foot. He walked along the dusty, lifeless road bordered on either side by towering walls of wire fencing stuffed tightly with straw—built to keep the enemy from seeing those passing through. Along the way, he could hear the battering of machine guns along the Vosges mountain range.

He passed village after village, remembering what was once beautiful and innocent, seeing now the wreckage of war. Houses destroyed by ceaseless shelling, street after street. *Where have the inhabitants gone? Are they still alive? Do they stand somewhere, alone, broken, and torn, like the homes they had to flee?*

Günsbach was the last unevacuated town before the jagged line of trenches marking the looming presence of war. As Albert got closer to his father's home, he had to wonder, *Is this the same idyllic village where I ran among the streets as an innocent child?* His mind journeyed back to a time now buried beneath the rubble of bombed-out houses and littered streets—a time of children playing with their friends, engaging in a friendly wrestling match.

Young Albert managed to wrestle down a bigger boy. Before he could savor the victory of having won, the older boy spitefully shouted, "Yes, if I got broth to eat twice a week, as you do, I should be as strong as you are!"[1] Albert quickly stood up, dusted himself off, and sadly made his way home. It had not previously been put into words, but now it had. He was different from the other boys. He was the son of a parson, a gentleman, and life was easier because of that.

As a normal boy, Albert wanted to fit in with the rest of the crowd. From that day onward, Albert made every effort to blend in with the boys. He refused to wear his new, warm overcoat that winter. None of the other boys had one, and he did not want to be seen as wealthier. He endured punishment for his insolence in refusing to wear the overcoat, proper gloves, or stylish hats and shoes, yet he did not back down. Even at a young age, his concern for people who had less was apparent. When others might have boasted of their differences from the less fortunate, he sought to be accepted as one of them.

After weaving through groups of soldiers milling about and past civilians picking up the pieces of their lives from the rubbled streets, Albert reached the vicarage. Even though it had been commandeered by German soldiers and officers, his father was still there, sitting stoically in his study. He no longer ran to the cellar for cover when bombs fell. He just sat there, as if he no longer cared whether he lived or died.

Albert's mother had been killed in 1916 when a troop of German cavalry raced down the road she was taking outside of town. She did not have time to move out of the way and was trampled to death by the galloping horses. Her death had not only devastated her husband, but Albert too.

Hélène soon joined Albert in Günsbach, and together they attempted to rebuild their lives from the fragments of their detainment in Africa, their internment in France, and their sorrows in his hometown.

The ravages of war. The destruction. The carnage. The seething hatred. The depths of sorrow and despair. All of it grieved Schweitzer, and he fell into a deep depression. His physical state had suffered ever since the short detainment at Bordeaux, where he was infected with dysentery. Throughout August, constant fatigue wore him down, and an intermittent fever fluctuated between moderate and severe. And he was beset with severe pain.

Schweitzer knew he needed medical attention. His wife accompanied him as he staggered toward Colmar, feeling every uneven step of the three miles they walked before a vehicle picked them up and drove them to Strasbourg. There, an operation performed by a Professor Stolz brought physical relief. Yet Albert's depression remained. Hélène also suffered from recurring fevers as well as extreme anxiety.

They sought peace among the hills. Albert remembered exploring them as a child, finding such joy in losing himself in the sights and sounds of nature. The hills still sloped gently upward, but the flowers and grass were gone, and only stumps remained of the spreading trees beneath which he once ran and played.

He recalled journeys with his mother, his three sisters, and his brother.

"My mother loved this path . . . this view. We rested among the flower-covered meadows, traveled deeper up the mountain trails until there was no longer a path and we were surrounded by the peaceful silence of nature." Albert sat down and wiped his heavy brow. Hélène sat next to him, her rounded tummy now showing signs of the life growing inside.

"We used to travel to Kaysersberg, the town where I was born under the shadow of that beautiful old castle. Outside the town, we walked through the valley until we came to a small mountain lake. My mother would sit down and close her eyes. She looked so peaceful as she would say, 'Here, children, I am completely at home. Here among the rocks, among the woods. I came here as a child. Let me breathe the fragrance of the fir trees and enjoy the quiet of this refuge from the world. Do not speak. After I am no longer on the earth, come here and think of me.'"[2]

Albert closed his eyes. "Now there is not even the song of the birds among these barren hills," he stated.

"It will grow again. Life will return once more." Hélène's smile brought with it a spark of hope.

"You are right, my dear. You are right."

———

Schweitzer received word from the mayor of Strasbourg, Mr. Schwander, asking if he would be interested in accepting a position as a doctor in Strasbourg. He was glad to accept the position and operated in the department for skin diseases. Once he returned to Strasbourg, Schweitzer was also reinstated as curator at the Church of St. Nicholas, where he had served for years. And he was allowed to stay at the parsonage since no one had been living there.

Dr. Schweitzer now had a residence and two vocations. Between his duties, he found time to once again take up the topic of philosophy, delving into the study of world religions, philosophies, and ethics.

The armistice in November 1918 did not bring great changes to his lifestyle. But when a new year dawned, the promise of God entered Albert's and Hélène's lives. They named her Rhena, and she was born on January 14, the same birthday as her father. Schweitzer continued his duties as doctor and pastor. The war had ended, and life, joy, and purpose began to infuse the land once more. Yet in his "seclusion at Strasbourg," Albert felt "rather like a coin that has rolled under a piece of furniture and has remained there lost."[3]

His mind often traveled back to his years in Lambaréné. Then he had known purpose, contentment, fulfillment. Now, he did not feel the strength or the motivation to journey down that path again. Would the time come to return to the people he had grown to love? He did not know. At the moment, other concerns pushed away such thoughts. His work as doctor covered only immediate expenses. And the war years in Lambaréné put Schweitzer so much in debt for the running of the hospital that it was a constant question in his mind how he would repay those debts.

His health was also a continued concern. In the summer, he underwent a second operation, which was to be the last, and soon he recovered.

The end of 1919 approached, and with it, an invitation that brought excitement to Schweitzer. It was four days before Christmas.

Albert joined his wife and their daughter as they walked in the garden. "Hélène, I received word from Upsala."

"Sweden?" Her face lit up with interest. "Do we know someone there?"

"The archbishop, Soderblom, has extended an invitation. He wants me to stay there during the spring of next year, to give lectures at the University of Upsala." He picked up his eleven-month-old daughter and swung her around. She giggled and grabbed at his moustache. "I have not been completely forgotten. Perhaps I do still have something to offer."

"Of course you do. You have so much to offer. I only wish . . ." Hélène's voice trailed off.

"What is it?"

"I only wish my health was better, that we could venture off once again into the unknown."

"Well, for now, Upsala will be enough adventuring for both of us. You have been invited as well. We are to stay with the archbishop."

"In his home? Oh, that will be wonderful!"

"Yes, it will. Now I only need to decide the topics of my lectures."

Schweitzer chose his favored topics of religion and philosophy, focusing on ethics and affirmation of life. He was somewhat at a loss without the manuscript he entrusted to the American missionary before leaving Lambaréné, but he threw himself into writing once more from his recollections.

The months in Upsala had a rejuvenating effect on Albert Schweitzer in more ways than one. The invigorating air and stimulating atmosphere merged together in a wonderful experience, almost as if the life-affirming topics of which he spoke found their way into his heart and brought him back to life as well. He enjoyed the academic climate at the university, especially his conversations with his students.

Almost before he knew it, Albert was walking up to the podium to give his final lecture in which he "developed the fundamental ideas of the ethic of Reverence for Life."[4]

As he spoke, he could sense that his words resonated in the hearts of those listening. All of them had faced difficult times. All were, in some way, members of the same brotherhood, bound together by the fellowship of pain. No individual life was untouched by the hardships of war, and the global implications of reverence for life touched Albert's soul deeper than ever. Tears filled his eyes, and for a moment, he could not speak. He had found healing for his heart and strength to pursue his destiny of ministering to mankind.

The archbishop and Albert walked together along the well-established grounds of Upsala University. "Your lectures were extremely successful."

"I have enjoyed them. I greatly appreciate your invitation to lecture here." Schweitzer's gratitude was sincere.

"What are your future plans now that this series of lectures is complete?"

"I have a financial burden that I must somehow be freed of. During the war years in Lambaréné, I incurred a fair amount of debt. I must repay the Paris Missionary Society, but I am unsure how to do so."

"As I said, many students here appreciated your lectures. Have you thought of doing more?"

"No, I had not really thought about it. I considered playing the organ, holding recitals."

"That is also a great talent with which you have been blessed."

"I owe my father for that. He started teaching me when I was only five, with my grandfather's old square piano. Even at that age, I delighted in improvising, creating harmonies rather than following the precise notes in the hymnal. I started playing the organ when I was eight. A year later, I was occasionally playing the organ during church services. When I was a young adult, my uncle made it possible for me to be tutored by Charles Marie Widor, the organist and composer."

"And the books you wrote with Widor, on Bach, set you apart as an organist in your own right." The archibishop spoke kindly. "You might consider both lectures and recitals."

"Perhaps." Albert's mind was intrigued at the possibilities. "Perhaps I shall."

And so he did. Within only three weeks of traveling throughout Sweden, holding organ concerts and delivering lectures, Albert Schweitzer brought in enough to pay off the majority of the hospital debts.

———

It was midsummer when Schweitzer returned to Strasbourg, renewed with vigor. And with vision. He was resolute. He would return to Lambaréné and resume his vocation as doctor to the people of Africa.

The remainder of the summer, Albert focused on writing

down memories of his first years in Lambaréné. Within the first year of its publication, *On the Edge of the Primeval Forest* had been translated into Swedish, German, and English from the original French. It was soon published in an additional four languages.

The year 1921 proved even more eventful than the previous one. On March 13, Schweitzer was in Spain, where he was thrilled to be the first organist to perform Bach's *St. Matthew Passion* in Barcelona.[5]

Albert finally received his long-awaited manuscript, yet found it difficult to focus on his work as doctor and pastor in addition to writing. He was confident of his ability to garner the needed funding for future work in Lambaréné—as well as current living expenses—through lectures, organ concerts, and royalties from his published works. So he resigned from his posts as doctor and preacher in Strasbourg, and the family resided at his father's simple vicarage in Günsbach.

Schweitzer traveled once more that autumn to Switzerland, and from there to Sweden. He then went to England to give a series of lectures, which took him to Oxford, Cambridge, Birmingham, and London, where between lectures he performed a number of organ recitals.

In the spring of 1922, Schweitzer returned to Sweden. From there, he traveled to Günsbach and enjoyed time with his wife and daughter. He had not been home long when the requests for concerts and lectures came once more from Switzerland, which took much of his time.

During the summer, Schweitzer enjoyed the opportunity to remain in Günsbach and continue his work of writing before again traveling to Switzerland in the fall. He delivered lectures at the university in Copenhagen and other towns of Denmark, interspersed with his organ concerts, where he brought the music of Bach to life in a way that no one had heard before or since.

January 1923 found Schweitzer in Prague, instructing again on the subject of his forthcoming book, *Philosophy of Civilization*. He greatly enjoyed traveling throughout Europe, delivering speeches, and giving recitals. He recalled that, when he prepared to leave for Africa, it was with the knowledge that he would be required to sacrifice three primary things—organ playing, teaching, and being able to support himself. Only a few close friends knew how difficult it was for him to let go of them.

The many evening hours he spent practicing Bach's works enabled Schweitzer to return to Europe with a honed skill that many held in high esteem. And though he had given up teaching in one university, requests streamed in for him to deliver lectures at many universities. By means of organ and pen, he was able to regain his financial security and, beyond that, to gather support for the upcoming years in Africa.

Also in 1923, his first two volumes of *Philosophy of Civilization* were published, *The Decay and Restoration of Civilization* as well as *Civilization and Ethics*. He then prepared for publishing *Christianity and the Religions of the World*—a collection of the lectures he gave in Birmingham.

As the landscape changed colorfully that fall, so did the landscape in Schweitzer's personal and professional life. It was time for a second sojourn in Africa. Hélène's health would not permit her to accompany her husband, and she remained in Europe with their daughter. But she gladly supported him in his decision to return. Albert was truly grateful for his wife's sacrifice, and her enthusiastic support for him to continue his work in Lambaréné gave him the focus he needed to finalize his preparations.

He packed cases of medicine and instruments through the winter of 1923–24, pausing to jot down a thought here, a memory there, writing one last book before his departure, which he completed shortly before he left. The idea originated during a trip to Zürich that summer. A friend of Schweitzer—the well-known psychoanalyst Dr. Oscar Pfister—encouraged him to rest awhile and leisurely share memories of his childhood. Dr. Pfister sent Schweitzer a copy of what he recorded during that one afternoon session, and it was the basis of his *Memoirs of Childhood and Youth*.

One Sunday, shortly before his departure, a blustery storm kept him indoors. And that is when he sat down to write a few last thoughts to add to his manuscript before submitting it to the printer:

> The most valuable knowledge we can have is how to deal with disappointments. All acts and facts are a product of spiritual power, the successful ones of power which is strong enough; the unsuccessful ones of power which is too weak. Does my behaviour in respect of love effect nothing? That is because there is not enough love in me. . . . Is my love of peace misunderstood and scorned? That means that I am not yet sufficiently peace-loving.[6]

He looked up from his manuscript and glanced outside the window. The rain had stopped, and a single ray of light beamed down from the gray sky. He turned to his manuscript once more: "No ray of sunlight is ever lost, but the green which it wakes into existence needs time to sprout, and it is not always granted to the sower to live to see the harvest. All work that is worth anything is done in faith."[7]

"Father," a small voice danced into the room.

"Yes, Rhena?" He laid down his pen and lifted his daughter onto his lap. "You're getting so big! I almost can't believe you are already five!"

"We had our birthdays on the same day, Father, you remember."

"Yes," he said with a laugh, "so we did, just a few weeks ago." His thoughts turned back the pages of the last few years, watching a darling baby grow into an even more darling child. He flipped forward to unwritten pages, where he would be waving good-bye, unsure of when he would see her again. He prayed it would not be long.

Rhena smiled and hopped down, running off to play, leaving Schweitzer once more with his thoughts. He thought of the world in which his daughter would grow up. In a world that seemed to be growing crueler than ever before, his concern was not only for her but for the future of mankind. He paused pensively, then took up his pen once more and continued writing:

As one who tries to remain youthful in his thinking and feeling . . . I still remain convinced that truth, love, peaceableness, meekness, and kindness are the violence which can master all other violence. . . .

All the kindness which a man puts out into the world works on the heart and the thoughts of mankind. . . . There is an unmeasured depth of truth in that strange saying of Jesus: "Blessed are the meek: for they shall inherit the earth" (Matt. 5:5).[8]

6

Living in Lambaréné

We are like waves that do not move individually but rise and fall in rhythm. To share, to rise and fall in rhythm with life around us, is a spiritual necessity.

—ALBERT SCHWEITZER

1924–27

Albert Schweitzer's second journey to Africa began on February 14, 1924, as he made his way from Strasbourg to Bordeaux. He was grateful for his traveling companion— Noel Gillespie—a young Oxford student whose mother had allowed him to leave for a few months to assist Schweitzer in his return to Lambaréné.

One week later, the Dutch cargo steamer *Orestes* carried them from the port of Bordeaux toward Africa. Schweitzer had stayed up all night, writing letters, hoping to post as many as possible before his departure. He still carried four sacks of mail, hoping to answer many more letters during the seven-week voyage to Cameroon. Schweitzer chose to travel by cargo boat, with its many stops, in order to have more time in which to answer.

As the sun scaled the heights above the receding landscape, his mind drifted back to the time when that same landscape had come into view. How quickly the years had gone! Could it be possible that he was finally returning to the place to which he had been called so long ago? It seemed hard to believe, yet it was true.

As the ship steamed toward open sea, and the shoreline disappeared, Schweitzer faced that open sea and the opportunities on the horizon. Gratefulness filled his heart at the thought of those who encouraged him in his return. Parishes across Europe—in Sweden, Denmark, England, Switzerland, and Czechoslovakia—had given support. Friends he had made during his years of lecturing and recitals also pledged their support. With the sun high in the sky and the steamer chugging toward its next stop of Dakar, Schweitzer retired to his room for a well-deserved rest.

On April 14, Schweitzer and his eighteen-year-old companion boarded a mail boat, *Europe*, the same vessel that had carried Albert and his wife to Africa eleven years before. Two days later, they arrived in Cape Lopez, also called Port Gentil.

"Doctor?" Hardly had he stepped onto the beach when the locals there flocked to him.

"Doctor!" a second person called.

"Our doctor has returned!" An enthusiastic group formed an impromptu welcoming committee even before he reached his final destination. After an overnight stay in Port Gentil, they boarded the *Alembe* to journey up the Ogowe River.

"This is the same boat we traveled on during our first voyage up the river," Dr. Schweitzer remarked to his young companion. "What a dirty old ramshackle boat it has become!"[1]

The next day, Good Friday, the silent river flowed past as the boat pressed its way toward Lambaréné. The small villages appeared aged, the people more ragged than before. The impoverished territory stood in sharp contrast to the more prosperous regions of the Gold Coast and the Cameroons, which they had just passed through.

Noel noticed this and asked Dr. Schweitzer the reason.

"They are poor because they are rich in valuable timber. The exploitation of the forests goes on at the expense of the cultivation of the means of life, and these have to be imported. So wherever we stop, we see the same sort of cargo unloaded: sacks of rice, cases of ship's biscuits, cases of dried fish, and, with these, casks of red wine."[2]

"So the natives pay a higher price for these imported items with the money they have earned through their work in the timber camps?"

"Yes, and at the same time, they neglect to cultivate their own fields and crops. It is a sad and vicious cycle, one that has continued for too long already."

Schweitzer turned again to his writing, and Noel watched the murky yellowish water flow by as they passed decrepit huts, papyrus swamps, and floating pirogues.

That evening at dinner, they were joined by a few timber merchants, some of whom Schweitzer knew from his previous years there. Conversation centered on prices of timber and labor, and then there was a lull until one experienced timber merchant spoke up.

"The leopard bands are spreading."

"Leopards?" Noel asked, somewhat nervously.

"They are not actual leopards," another man explained. "They are leopard men, belonging to secret bands that roam and bring terror with their murdering. They tie a leopard's claws on their hands and feet—or iron replications of them—and kill men."

"Why?"

"Some of these men did not willingly become members of the band. A man is offered a drink, but this drink has been spiked with a bit of magic potion," the timber merchant replied.

"Of course we know there is no such thing as a potion with magical powers," Dr. Schweitzer interrupted. He remembered these bands from his years in Africa and shuddered to think that they had expanded their territory. "These men are superstitious. They are told that they have drunk a potion mixed in a human skull, a mixture made with the blood of another victim, and that they are now under its power. Now that man is also a member of the band and must also kill like a leopard."

"I still don't see the reason for the killings," Noel persisted.

"The beliefs of the tribesmen go deep," Schweitzer explained. "The medicine men and elders do not wish to lose their influence over the young men. They use this as a way to keep the men in strict allegiance to their ancient beliefs and to instill fear in the hearts of the others. Those targeted are the ones who have forsaken their loyalties to the old ways or those who have converted to Christianity."

All fell silent again. After the pause, Schweitzer said, "If you will excuse me, gentlemen, I believe some fresh night air is in order."

He walked through the swaying boat and stepped out onto the deck. The moon was full, its shimmering reflection dancing on the surface of the water, broken by shadows of tree branches reaching over the river. On such a perfect night, illuminated by the Easter moon, Schweitzer found it hard to believe that beneath its blanket lurked such terror and grief caused by superstition and fanaticism.[3]

The following morning, as the sun's rays filtered through the trees and reflected off the water, they arrived at Lambaréné. No canoes had yet shown up from the mission station. Even when they had, it was a challenge to find enough canoes for all the crates, packages, and belongings that Schweitzer carried.

It was midday when, as if in a dream, Schweitzer stepped onto the shore.

"Noel, please keep track of the unloading," he said to his assistant. "I must see the hospital grounds." As he walked toward the hills, Schweitzer realized that the forest had reclaimed the compound. Long grass sprouted from every corner, and brushwood grew where buildings once stood. Only the two buildings made of corrugated iron were still standing, although the palm leaf roofing was damaged beyond repair.

One of the missionaries, Mr. Herrmann, joined Schweitzer as he rediscovered his hospital quarters. "Monsieur Pelot and I made every effort to keep the roofs in repair. We worked on them after every wet season, but over the past year our own duties have taken up all our time. We could not keep up with them as well."

"Not to worry. There is much to be done, and that is why I am here." Schweitzer was overwhelmed by nostalgia as he made his way toward his small doctor's house. The path was so overgrown he could hardly recognize it.

"First thing tomorrow morning, I will send the boys to clear this walkway to your quarters," Mr. Herrmann assured the doctor.

"Oh no," Schweitzer answered, "let me tread it clear again."[4]

"Yes, but first, let us have lunch."

Albert was pleased to be reunited with some of the same missionaries and teachers he had known from before. They enjoyed a simple lunch, and talk soon turned to the work that needed to be done for the hospital.

"I heard from a few carpenters. They wrote me and said they would be available to help in the rebuilding process." Although the buildings were in a greater state of disrepair than he had imagined, he was hopeful and ready to begin the work.

"You will be hard-pressed to find them, Doctor," Mr. Herrmann responded. "Timber merchants everywhere are preparing for a couple of international exhibitions; they've received orders from all over the world and are hiring anyone available who can hold an axe."

"Well, perhaps the rebuilding can wait. But those two main buildings need the roofing repaired. I believe the first task at hand is to procure thatched roof tiles." After lunch, Schweitzer traversed the length of the Lambaréné village, but he didn't find so much as a shingle.

The common response he received was, "Look at our own roofs; no one has the time to stitch raffia leaves over bamboo." They were right; Schweitzer's buildings were not the only ones lacking proper roofs.

"Noel, do you care to join me?"

"Where to, Doctor?"

"A nearby village, a little over an hour's journey. They

know me well. Perhaps I can find some roofing material there."

In that village, Schweitzer was greeted by many who fondly remembered Le Grand Docteur. He wandered from hut to hut, greeting old acquaintances, at the same time keeping his eyes out for roof tiles. After expressing his need, he was led to a hut, behind which lay twenty roof tiles. After a few more findings, he had gathered sixty-four of them.

"How much can I pay you for these leaf tiles?" Schweitzer asked.

"Oh, these are not for sale," an elderly man replied.

"We need them for our own village," another one added.

Schweitzer persisted: "I have returned to rebuild the hospital and need these to repair my roofs. Otherwise I will not be able to treat people. I will pay you well, and I have gifts in my canoe."

"There is another village, upriver a few miles," said one of the villagers. "Perhaps you will find some there."

"If you would like *your* people to be treated at the hospital," Schweitzer countered craftily, "please let me buy your roof tiles."

The men around him laughed. "Our good doctor would never refuse treatment to anyone." Schweitzer's widely known compassion did not assist him in his bargaining. But the negotiations continued, and the doctor did not give up. As a heavy rain started to fall, and the sun sank beneath the green canopy, Schweitzer and Noel loaded sixty-four leaf tiles into their canoe and were rowed back to Lambaréné.

=====

The first weeks were filled with unpacking and restocking, repairing roofs, and reclaiming the grounds from the forest. All the while, Schweitzer was treating the sick, who started arriving almost as soon as the doctor returned to Lambaréné. The consulting room and dispensary were repaired first, followed by the patients' ward. Schweitzer returned in the middle of the rainy season, and recovering patients, whose immune systems were already weakened, succumbed easily to chills caused by rain pouring through gaping holes in the roof. Because of that, even to the neglect of their other duties, Noel or Dr. Schweitzer was often seen climbing aboard a canoe in search of roof tiles. This single undertaking required time and great expense, yet it was a life-or-death necessity.

Once these first buildings were in satisfactory condition, Schweitzer undertook the construction of another building to be used for storage of equipment, building materials, and the washing boiler. It was no small task, for he found that the family members of his current patients had no foresight regarding those who would come to the hospital in the months and years to come. They had no interest in putting forth the effort to create comfortable living arrangements for future patients:

> I . . . have to play myself the part of building-superinten-
> dent, routing the people out every morning from behind
> their cooking-pots, flattering them, promising them
> food and presents, forcing the tools into their hands, and

in the evening seeing that all the axes, hatchets, bush-knives, and all unused material have been brought back.

Sometimes I have half a dozen workers, sometimes a couple; often when I come down in the morning I cannot find a single one. They have gone fishing, or have left to visit their village and get a supply of food, or they had to go somewhere to take part in a great palaver. Then the work is at a standstill for days.[5]

Meanwhile, patients appeared on a daily basis. Within two months, the hospital accommodated more than twenty patients suffering from sleeping sickness, a similar number of those affected with leprosy, and twice as many suffering from ulcers, heart complaints, and injuries from accidents. The wards were stretched to the limit with close to one hundred patients.

Treatment for victims of sleeping sickness required a six-week stay—for those who had been diagnosed early enough to be treated. Others were in the later stages of the disease and little could be done, except to make them comfortable. Those with sleeping sickness, as well as those with ulcers, needed regular injections. For the average patient, this single task was difficult. For the malnourished victims of sleeping sickness—some of whom resembled skeletons—it was nearly impossible to find a vein in which to inject the medicine.

One afternoon, Schweitzer returned to the hospital after another foray along the villages of the river, seeking roof tiles. There, lying a few feet from the doorway, a figure could be seen. At closer observation, Schweitzer found an old man, shivering with little clothing and no other belongings. He glanced up at the doctor, who quickly called for Noel to help carry him inside.

"Who brought you here?" Schweitzer asked. He often saw patients beyond hope of recovery, deposited upon the shore or at the hospital door to be cared for by "the good doctor." Their only hope of relief was through death.

"I have rich relatives. They are near Samkita. They will come soon, with food, and a gift . . . for you." The man's dull eyes barely focused as he repeated his promise to Dr. Schweitzer.

"I will find you a blanket." Schweitzer had great difficulty locating both a blanket and mosquito netting for his unexpected patient.

Noel found mosquito netting, and he was able to secure a blanket from the storage room. "We desperately need supplies," Noel confided to Schweitzer.

"I shipped seventy-three cases from Strasbourg, months ago. They should arrive soon." Schweitzer could only hope and pray that they would. He returned to the old man, placing a blanket on his emaciated body.

"My relatives will come soon. They will reward you and bring supplies for me." The man was insistent. Schweitzer smiled down at him in appreciation and ensured he was comfortable before leaving the ward. Noel followed him.

"Do you think he really does have relatives?"

"If he had," Schweitzer observed, "would they have dropped him off with barely a strip of clothing? No, I do not expect anyone to come for him. The best thing we can do for him now is to listen to him and act as if we believe his statements."

"The hospital is becoming a place where they deposit the dying"—Noel's words were intense—"expecting us to care for them and feed them, even for weeks or months, until they die."

"It is a burden," Schweitzer agreed, "especially as there is no separate ward for terminal cases. Just last week three patients left the hospital after watching one such hopeless case pass from this world."

"What are we to do?" Noel asked.

"We are to care for them and treat them with dignity. This hospital is open to all who suffer, no matter their state. We will not be able to save them all from death, but if we can ease their suffering and let them feel our love and compassion, I believe we have succeeded."

Not long afterward, this man passed away, as did a woman who was brought to the hospital in a similar state. Monsieur Herrmann, the missionary, spoke at the funeral held for her.

"Here lies a woman who, in the time she was most in need of help, was cast off by her own people. Yet she was welcomed by strangers and shown tenderness and compassion. Because Jesus' love has come into the world, people in despair now have hope."

A shaft of sunlight angled through the palm trees as a small group of children from the mission school sang at the woman's grave. Everyone gathered there felt the warmth of the sun and the love of Christ that constrained them to reach out to those in need and give them hope when no one else would.[6]

Dr. Schweitzer had begun to dread the noon hour, when patients or their attendants gathered around the consulting room to request rations. As before, the patients' family members cooked for themselves in an open cooking area near the main hospital ward. The daily rations consisted of a pound of rice, six or more large bananas, or several sticks of manioc "bread."[7] He also dispensed palm oil or imported cooking fat from Europe. After a successful fishing expedition, he supplied fish.

Daily rations were given to those who arrived from a long distance, to those who required a long hospital stay and did not have supplies, and to those who provided labor for Dr. Schweitzer. However, each day people approached the storage house who did not fall within those categories. Perhaps they worked one day, fell sick the next day, and hoped to work again soon; thus they expected a ration. Reasons and excuses were varied and vast, and Schweitzer had a difficult time turning anyone away. He finally turned to a new aide, a local man named G'Mba, who enthusiastically embraced every task given him. He took up this new task of distributing rations with wisdom, and Schweitzer was greatly relieved.

═══

Construction of a second ward had begun, yet it had to cease for a few weeks to allow for the hasty building of a cell for mental patients. A young mental patient—who suffered from a late stage of sleeping sickness—had become dangerous and needed to be restrained in a safe place. Noel undertook this latest task and was dismayed that the patient always found the weakest place in the building. For ten days he broke out each evening. At last the cell was complete.

The following day, the ground beneath Noel gave way as he stood in the coop counting chickens. The walls collapsed upon themselves, calling for a second urgent construction project, before wild animals could make off with the precious poultry.

The first day of summer proved promising. The long-awaited shipment of cases arrived as well as the Lambaréné mission's first motorboat, which was at once used in transporting Schweitzer's seventy-three cases of equipment upriver to the hospital.

One month later, another arrival lightened the loads that Schweitzer and Noel had been carrying. Mathilde Kottmann, a nurse from Strasbourg, immediately went to work. She took over the myriad kitchen duties—boiling water, counting fowls, planning meals, finding eggs, as well as assuming the responsibility of the weekly washing. Once everything was running smoothly on those fronts, she devoted any extra time to the hospital.

Joseph, Schweitzer's first assistant, returned to Lambaréné and began to work for the hospital once more, although his other vocation in the timber trade took him away from time to time.

A month following Mrs. Kottmann's arrival, it was time for Noel to depart. His assistance was sorely missed. Keeping up with the tasks of both doctor and builder had become more than one man could adequately bear. Yet Dr. Schweitzer did not have to wait long before help arrived.

Victor Nessmann, a young doctor also from Alsace, made it possible for Dr. Schweitzer to focus more aptly on the construction projects while Nessmann stood in the gap at the hospital. Upon his arrival, he greeted Dr. Schweitzer by saying, "Now you shall rest, and I will take over all the work."[8]

The young doctor proved himself true to that statement over the subsequent weeks. Schweitzer commented that his new assistant, who was organized and practical, yet bestowed with an essential sense of humor, was made for Africa.[9]

By that time, the rainy season had begun, but frequent downpours had already come throughout the dry season of May through September. Crops and vegetation deteriorated under the intermittent rain, and Schweitzer's concern was for the year ahead. *How will the country survive if there's a famine?*

A third doctor, Mark Lauterburg, joined the Lambaréné team in the spring of 1925. His help was invaluable in a hospital overflowing from an unrelenting stream of patients. He took charge of surgeries, which earned him the title "the man who cuts boldly" by the local people.

In early summer, one timber camp after another succumbed to dysentery attacks. It soon flared into an epidemic that raged through the entire region. Although Schweitzer continued construction of one building after another, the grounds were too small to expand. Wards built for no more than forty patients were housing twice that number, and despite efforts to keep the affected patients separate from other patients, the dysentery spread.

The famine, caused by the continued rains of the previous year, hit Lambaréné by autumn. It began in the summer, but imported rice kept the hospital running, for a time anyway. Those supplies stopped unexpectedly when a shipment carrying thousands of tons of rice was wrecked on the African coast. The rice was ruined. Schweitzer had foreseen a shortage and stocked up on rice during the summer, which allowed them to survive during the difficult months.

By October, Schweitzer had reached a decision. At the present location, the hospital had no way to expand. There was space for 50 patients, but more than 125 currently stayed in the wards. Food was a daily concern. In a different location, there would be opportunity to grow crops and plant trees to become somewhat self-sufficient. With these points in mind, he met with his hospital staff of three doctors and two nurses. Every member of the staff had felt the burden of cramped and inconvenient quarters.

He shared with them a possible solution: building a new hospital community on a flat-topped hill a couple of miles up the Ogowe River. The new location had the name of *Adolinanango*, Bantu for "looking out over the peoples."[10] The staff was overjoyed at the news of the hospital's expansion.

Although he had hoped to return to Europe at the beginning of 1926, Schweitzer knew that no one else could supervise the enormous building project. He was willing to make the sacrifices necessary, and work commenced. Throughout 1926, amidst overwhelming hospital duties, the new hospital community was constructed.

On January 21, 1927, the patients were transported to

their new wards—spacious and clean. By evening, Schweitzer brought up the last of the patients, those with mental disorders, who would live in rooms with wooden floors rather than the moist earth of their former cells.

Schweitzer made sure they were comfortable before returning along the winding path down the hill upon which the hospital was situated. From every fireside and beneath every mosquito netting, people called out with joy: "This is a good hut, doctor, a good hut!"[11]

At last—fourteen years after he arrived in Africa—the doctor could provide proper accommodation for his patients. Joy overwhelmed him as he looked up into the clear night sky, grateful to the God who had provided for him thus far, who bestowed upon him the abilities to undertake such a massive project, and who touched the hearts of friends across Europe to supply funding for the efforts.

"It is a pretty good hut." Schweitzer smiled to himself as he turned into his own quarters.

7

Living Between Two Worlds

Heavy is the burden of fatigue and responsibility which has lain upon me without a break for years. I have not much of my life for myself, not even hours I should like to devote to my wife and child. But I have had blessings, too; that I am allowed to work in the service of mercy; that my work has been successful; that I receive from other people affection and kindness in abundance.

—ALBERT SCHWEITZER

1927–39

Once again on board a steamer, the rugged green landscape shrinking before the azure sky and cerulean sea, Dr. Schweitzer departed the African coast. It was July 1927, and it had been three and a half years since he last saw his wife and daughter. During this long sojourn to Africa, Schweitzer's father had also passed away in 1925 at the age of 80.

During the six months since the relocation to the new hospital site, building had continued. The community now had the capability of housing between 200 and 250 patients and their companions, if necessary. The usual number of patients had been between 140 and 160.

With the hospital operating smoothly and a couple of doctors to fill in during his absence, Dr. Schweitzer returned to his homeland for a two-year furlough.

His reunion with his wife and eight-year-old daughter was long overdue. His heart filled with joy at the thought of seeing them again. Yet joy mingled with the sorrow from leaving Africa and the people there whom he had grown to love.

The two years in Europe would not be devoted only to rest and writing. Schweitzer spent much of his time traveling.

Individuals from Sweden to Denmark, from Holland to England, from Switzerland to Germany to Czechoslovakia benefited from his poignant lectures and passionate recitals.

He spent the most precious moments with his wife and daughter in a peaceful resort at Konigsfeld, northern Germany. In the fresh mountain air, Hélène found her health improving, so her husband maintained a home there for his small family. He took advantage of any quiet moments to continue writing, this time attempting to complete his book, *The Mysticism of Paul the Apostle*, which he had begun before his first journey to Africa yet never found time to complete. Page by page, it came together, as did his plans for the next stay in Lambaréné.

The time had come once more to leave. A month before his fifty-fifth birthday, Schweitzer boarded a ship bound for Cape Lopez. He was not alone. His wife traveled with him, as did Dr. Anna Schmitz and Marie Secretan, who volunteered to help. During his two-year stay in Europe, he encouraged others to help with the work in Lambaréné, and four doctors from Switzerland had followed the call of service to the people of Africa.

Schweitzer took full advantage of the long voyage to complete his book on Saint Paul, writing the last chapter en route to Cape Lopez along with the preface as the steamer chugged up the Ogowe River. They arrived at Lambaréné a few days after Christmas 1929.

The year of 1930 was occupied with further construction as the quarters proved to be too small due to a second dysentery epidemic.

By 1931, though, Dr. Schweitzer's fortitude paid off in

the way of a unique, effective, and sustainable hospital community, to meet the ever-growing needs of the surrounding villages. With the help and support of friends overseas, the hospital had a fully equipped operating theater, a dispensary stocked with every necessary medication, and a storage shed that supplied food for not only the staff but also patients who could not provide for themselves.

Schweitzer's humility was apparent in his words as he gave credit not to himself for spearheading and taking up the bulk of the work in Lambaréné over a period of many years, but to others: "How can we thank sufficiently the friends of the hospital who have made such a work possible!"[1]

He also strived toward making the hospital sustainable in itself by growing fruits, vegetables, and grains on the hospital grounds:

> Year after year . . . work has been carried on with the object of producing a Garden of Eden round the hospital. Hundreds of young fruit trees, which we have grown from pips, have already been planted. Some day there must be so much fruit growing here that all can take what they please, and there will no longer be such a crime as stealing. We have already got to that stage with the fruits of the papaya, the mango trees, and the oil palms.[1]

The design of the hospital merged practicality with comfort. Each building was erected on eighteen- to twenty-inch wooden piles to keep them from flooding during the rainy season. They were built of mahogany, a local wood with grain so tight that not even termites could damage it. The hospital complex could rightfully be dubbed a village, with dozens of buildings, barns, paths, groves, plantations, and a landing on the river's edge.

In 1931, during his third stay in Africa, Schweitzer responded to a publisher's plea for an autobiography.

"If you don't write it, someone else will," Felix Meiner persisted.

Schweitzer felt that at his relatively young age, he did not have enough experience to compose an autobiography.

"You could at least write regarding the development of your thoughts and experiences up to this point in your life," his wife suggested.

Schweitzer acquiesced and took up the project. Within a month, during which Schweitzer left the operating of the hospital to his competent coworkers, he completed the manuscript for *Out of My Life and Thought*, published first in Leipzig, Germany, in 1931, followed by an edition in England in 1932 and one in America in 1933. Nearly half a million copies were printed, and the royalties from Schweitzer's books aided the hospital's operating expenses.

The next decade saw Schweitzer truly a man of the world, with frequent trips carrying him from Africa to Europe and back again. He spent as much time as possible with his wife and growing daughter, yet frequently received requests from churches, missionary conferences, universities, medical societies, and seminaries across the continent. The 30s brought with it a depression that was global in its reach, and donations from individuals to support the hospital decreased; thus it was necessary for him to deliver lectures and organ recitals. It was work but also a great source of joy for him.

In February 1932, when Schweitzer was in Europe, he became aware of darkening shadows that had begun to lengthen acrosss the world, threatening a second war. Yet many people seemed to be closing their consciences to the evils that lurked in the shadows.

At that time Schweitzer received an invitation to Frankfurt, Germany, to speak at the centennial celebration honoring Goethe's death. Johann Wolfgang von Goethe— German philosopher, writer, biologist, and artist—influenced the thought and philosophy of Albert Schweitzer, who had extensively studied his works. He wished to emulate one of Goethe's mottos: "Do good for the pure love of doing good."[2]

In part, Schweitzer's speech consisted of a call for what it means to be fully and boldly human:

> Goethe's message to the men of today is the same as to the men of his time and to the men of all times: "Strive for true humanity. Become yourself a man who is true to his inner nature, a man whose deed is in tune with his character." . . . Can we still achieve such humanity in the midst of the frightful circumstances of our day? . . .

Now, a hundred years after his death it has come to pass, through a calamitous development determined by events . . . that the material and spiritual independence of the individual, so far as it is not already destroyed, is most seriously threatened. . . . To the individual [Goethe] says: Do not abandon the ideal of personality even when it runs counter to developing circumstances. . . . Remain men, in possession of your own souls. Do not become human beings which have offered hospitality to souls which conform to the will of the masses and beat in time with it.[3]

The meaning behind his speech was clearly understood by Germans nationwide. Many who were already loyal to the Nazis' beliefs were angered by his words. Others agreed with him, yet feared speaking up when the country was precariously close to the chasm of another war. As Schweitzer left Germany and continued traveling through Europe, he received letters from acquaintances and friends in Germany. Schweitzer was greatly disappointed to see that a large number of the letters were from pastors and other religious leaders. They expressed their fear of speaking up or taking a particular side in the perilous political climate. Given the chance to stand up for peace and truth, many opted instead for silence. Schweitzer canceled his speaking engagements in Germany and did not return there until after Hitler's death and the end of World War II.

After nearly a year in Africa, from April 1933 to February 1934, Schweitzer returned to Europe. More and more, he found his philosophy at odds with that of the world climate, a fact that caused him deep concern. Rather than choose despair, he continued to make his life the greatest argument for his philosophical beliefs. Through his personal example as well as his speeches throughout Europe, he spoke of "the necessity of aid to the Africans, not as benevolence but as a duty."[4]

He continued to stress that the vital need of mankind was to develop a deep reverence for all forms of life and that the change required across the world had to come from the depths of the human heart rather than through mere rhetoric.

After his fifth period in Africa, which was only a six-month stay, Schweitzer returned to Europe. Due to political and economic instability in Germany—a main source of support for the hospital—contributions dwindled drastically. He remained in Europe for nearly a year and a half. He had relocated his European dwelling from the mountain village of Konigsfeld, Germany, to Lausanne, Switzerland. Because his wife's ancestry was Jewish, and his own stance clearly opposed to the prevailing racial attitudes of Germany, he thought it safer to stay out of harm's way in a more neutral country.

In February 1937, Schweitzer returned once more to Africa, and he worked there throughout that year and 1938. During those same years, Schweitzer's wife and their daughter made a couple of journeys of their own to the United States. Hélène had a number of speaking engagements, sharing the burdens and joys of the work in Lambaréné and the needs of the hospital and its patients. The result of those visits was the formation of an organization that exists to this day: the Albert Schweitzer Fellowship (www.schweitzerfellowship.org).

═══

The Schweitzer-Bresslau (Mrs. Schweitzer's maiden name was Bresslau) Hospital bustled with life as foreigners and locals interacted in a place unique from any other in the world. Villagers from the farthest reaches of the country felt at home during their recovery, as did ailing foreigners, each one receiving individualized attention and professional care. Whether walking down the paths that were bathed with sunlight, or sitting at the landing that was alive with colorful people, animals, and clothing, one would hear a sampling of half a dozen languages. Local dialects of Bapunu and people from other tribes, in addition to French, German, and English all came together in a strange but oddly harmonious blend.

It was a turbulent time for Africans, finding the need to transition from the primitive way of their ancestors to a more modern, Westernized way of life. It affected every sphere of their existence—social, cultural, and economic. Dr. Schweitzer opposed many of the evils that colonialism introduced, such as exploitation and slavery. At the same time, he did not know whether the people of Africa, so recently forced into the throes of a morphing postwar world, would be ready for self-government. For the most part, though, Schweitzer was not vocal about this in the country he served, choosing to focus his energies instead on the urgent needs of his hospital.

A letter penned on Palm Sunday to friends in Europe

makes it clear that his thoughts were never far from the darkening sky looming over the places he once called home:

> Even though I am working, my thoughts are in Jerusalem. . . . What happened there—the entrance of the Lord—is, for me, the prelude to something that has to come someday: the beginning of the Kingdom of God. I feel alienated from the whole new trend of ideas because all these people no longer carry within them the idea of the Kingdom of God. . . . We must be the people who preserve true thought for a time to come. How well I now understand the prophets who, in the time of the coming and the destruction of Jerusalem, thought about and looked forward to the subsequent future, transcending the present. That is how Palm Sunday should be.[5]

After two demanding and eventful years in Africa, Schweitzer returned to Europe in early February 1939 and found that the winds of war were gathering strength, threatening to sweep across the shores of Europe. Schweitzer knew his place was among the people of Africa. He would not leave them this time if he could at all help it. Twelve days after arriving in Europe, he boarded the same ship by which he had come and returned to to Africa.

8

Little Miracles in Lambaréné

The purpose of existence is that we human beings, all nations and the whole of humanity, should constantly progress toward perfection. We must search for these conditions and hold fast to these ideals. If we do this, our finite spirit will be in harmony with the infinite.

—Albert Schweitzer

1939–44

chweitzer sauntered through the spreading mango grove early one morning. Other than the cheerful greetings of the birds and the distant gurglings of the river, it was quiet. His mind was cluttered with tasks. His first task upon returning to Africa had been to order medical equipment, pharmaceuticals, and other health-related supplies from both Africa and Europe. Most arrived promptly, for which he was grateful. He then ordered a three-year stock of staple foods, mainly rice, hoping it would last until the war ended.

Beneath the peaceful canopy of the mango trees, it was hard to imagine that war had begun. Although Schweitzer stayed as far away from the conflict as possible, he found himself once again caught between German and French lines. To the north, the side of the Vichy French—under the Axis powers—was based out of Cameroon. The Free French forces—supported by the Allied powers—approached from the south. *When will opposing armies meet? And where?*

It did not take long to find out. The line of engagement stretched the length of the Ogowe River. Along its shores, countless clashes were fought. The hospital grounds were respected as a no-combat zone. Even so, war planes were often seen soaring overhead as the conflict drew closer.

Schweitzer's main obligation lay where it always had: tending the needs of the sick and injured. The hospital doors remained open to all, regardless of what side they supported or for whom they fought. With the added strain of treating war victims, supplies dwindled. At the same time, the staff fell to three doctors, including Dr. Schweitzer, and four nurses—the lowest number in many years.

The second year after his return to Africa, 1940, drew to a close.

Although mail was erratic, when the mail boat arrived from Port Gentil, Schweitzer took a canoe the couple of miles down to the main village of Lambaréné.

"Dr. Schweitzer, here is a letter for you."

A smile spread across his face as he read the contents. He folded it and placed it in his pocket, heading back up to the hospital.

"I received a letter today," Dr. Schweitzer spoke to his staff at supper. All eyes turned to the doctor.

"You are aware that my wife spent some time in the United States before the war began. It seems that some of those to whom she spoke have mobilized their efforts to aid us. They have formed a group, calling themselves the Albert Schweitzer Fellowship, and they have contacted me, inviting us to send them a list. They will do their best to send us the supplies we need."

Expressions of joy and relief sounded around the room, and they immediately began to write a letter of appreciation as well as draw up a lengthy list of needs.

They waited in anticipation for the shipment throughout 1941. Supplies from Europe had completely ceased for the time being; the American group's supplies were their only hope for keeping the hospital in operation.

Summer 1941 held another pleasant surprise. On August 2, a dearly missed member of the Schweitzer staff returned to Lambaréné following a long absence. She traveled south through the war-torn countries of Europe, crossing into Lisbon, Portugal. From there she took a ship to Angola, six hundred miles south of Lambaréné. Her safe arrival was truly miraculous after such a risky journey.

Hélène Schweitzer had finally joined her husband in Lambaréné. Their reunion marked a high point during the challenging war years. No signs pointed to an imminent end of the war, yet with the arrival of his beloved wife and daughter, his spirits were high.

Toward the end of the year, the shipment from the States finally arrived. The drugs and medical supplies would enable the hospital to continue running. What brought even more joy were the unexpected items, such as a pair of gloves that actually fit Schweitzer's large hands, and cooking utensils.

Yearly shipments followed from the faithful members of the Albert Schweitzer Fellowship. The shipment of 1942 made it possible for the hospital to accept new patients. Their minimal supplies meant that they had been able to care only for patients currently receiving treatment.

The shipment of 1943 included not only medical supplies, but also eyeglasses and shoes, which they distributed to grateful patients. At the close of the day, Schweitzer took out his journal. "How grateful I am," he wrote, "to faithful friends in the countries that have helped me, for now I can take in all the sick who are in great need. We are greatly encouraged in our work!"[1]

The needs escalated through the war years. Operating conditions were even more difficult than those of the first war. Nevertheless, help always arrived at just the right time. These little miracles assured Schweitzer and the staff that their efforts were blessed by God.

Writing to an acquaintance in Europe during the fall of 1943, Schweitzer provided details of the daily operations at the Lambaréné hospital:

In June I sent my young colleague on vacation that he might relax a bit; throughout these months I have been doing all the work in the hospital on my own, helped only by Dr. Wildikann. . . . She takes care of the women and children and I the men, urology, and surgery. I'm very happy to be doing operations again, to which I devote two and sometimes three mornings a week. There is so much to do here in surgery, especially in regard to hernias and elephantiasis tumors. Luckily, we still have material for operations. I spent two hours a day overseeing the workers in the garden and the plantation and directing the two carpenters who are still busy maintaining and repairing the many hospital buildings. . . . At present my wife is spending a brief holiday at the seashore. It is a blessing that I can endure the infamous jungle climate so well.[2]

The rains did not cease during the dry season of 1944, making it impossible to grow manioc, bananas, and other crops. Schweitzer was deeply concerned for the following year, knowing that a famine could easily occur, especially with the present conditions of war and a struggling economy.

January 14, 1945, was Albert Schweitzer's seventieth birthday. In a letter to the General Council of Congregational Churches in the United States, he expressed his gratefulness for their support, as well as some personal thoughts on his recently passed birthday:

> For what I have to do and for a long time, it might be good for the hospital if I could go on directing it, I ought to be thirty and not seventy years old. But it is a great privilege that at seventy I am still able to do the necessary [work]. Every day I realize with profound gratitude toward God the grace that at my age I can still do my work in the African jungle. By the great gift, which the telegram announces and to which you have so generously contributed, I am stirred with emotion and I thank you from the depth of my heart. This magnificent present will find good use. It will help to nourish the many single sick in my hospital who have come from afar and don't possess anything. . . . And very often they have to stay here for weeks, even for months. I feel so sorry if I have to send away a patient who has not quite fully recovered, in order to economize the food which I am obliged to give him. Your wonderful gift frees me of much [anxiety] of that kind. This is a glorious feeling for me, to

whom deliverance [from] such [anxiety] gives back fresh courage.[3]

———

Monday, May 7, 1945, began as a normal day filled with the usual hospital duties. During lunch, Schweitzer had been contemplating his replies to the most pressing communication before the steamer departed at two o'clock. After lunch, he sat at his desk writing when a patient appeared at his window.

"The radio station in Leopoldville just transmitted a German bulletin. They will be concluding an armistice, on land and at sea!"

The words didn't fully sink in, but Schweitzer quickly completed his letters, then walked down to the hospital to treat his patients. Afterward, the hospital bell was rung vigorously, and it was announced to all that the war was over. Still, the reality of the news hadn't affected him, and he continued his daily duties, wearily making his way to the plantation to check on the workers.

At last, upon retreating to his quarters that evening, Schweitzer began to consider the implications of the war's ending. Day after day, the information he received about the war caused him great distress. The starvation and mistreatment of thousands in prison camps; the plight of the Jews, Polish, Dutch, Christians, and others who fell under the merciless hands of the Nazis; the suffering of thousands of refugees across Europe—all these had weighed heavily upon his heart.

Now it was over. He breathed deeply as he thought of people who, for the first time in so many months, would sleep without the fear of bombings or other horrors during the night. Listening to the soft rustling of the lofty palms outside his window, he turned to his bookshelf and pulled out an ancient book, *The Sayings of Lao-tse*, which recorded the thoughts of a Chinese philosopher of the sixth century BC. The words written thousands of years before poignantly spoke to the world of today:

> Weapons are disastrous implements, no tools for a noble being. Only when he cannot do otherwise, does he make use of them. Quiet and peace are for him the highest. He conquers, but he knows no joy in it. He who would rejoice in victory, would be rejoicing in murder. At the victory celebration, the general should take his place as is the custom at a funeral ceremony. The slaughter of human beings in great numbers should be lamented with tears of compassion. Therefore should he, who has conquered in battle, bear himself as if he were at a festival of mourning.[4]

He closed the small book and returned it to its place. The war was over, and that was the good news. The bad news was that the world would never be the same. The very weapon that had ended global hostilities ushered in an era of global uncertainties.

After the war, Schweitzer and his wife remained in Lambaréné. Mathilde Kottmann, a nurse who had been stranded in Alsace during the war years, returned as soon as the conflict ended. The other members of the hospital staff returned to their respective countries, and the staff consisted of only Schweitzer, his wife, and the faithful nurse.

By autumn 1945, the effects of the previous year's rains became apparent. Crops failed. Prices soared. They found themselves once again caught in the throes of famine.

One year later, after trying to operate the hospital under such dire conditions, Schweitzer was on the verge of defeat. He had just opened a letter and discovered, to his chagrin, that the hospital owed the local bank, Banque Commerciale Africaine, a debt of 124,752 francs [$1,045 in 1945]. It would be impossible to repay the debt, at the moment anyway. The small amount of money they had was needed for living and operating expenses.

"We will have to close the hospital." What Schweitzer feared and fought against for so long had come upon him at last. The unwelcome realization tolled through his mind with resounding finality.

Trying to keep from being overcome by despair, he opened one last letter. It was in a small unmarked envelope. *Probably a letter from some villager requesting medication*, Schweitzer thought.

Instead, it was from the director of a new bank, planning to open an agency in Port Gentil (formerly called Cape Lopez): "I am pleased to inform you that I am holding, for the disposal of the Schweitzer-Bresslau Hospital, the amount of

380,822 francs [$4,375 in 1945] from the Unitarian Service Committee in the United States."[5]

His heart pounded. He reread the letter, reread it again. The hospital was saved!

Schweitzer almost floated his way from the Lambaréné Post Office back toward the landing, when he heard his name called.

"Dr. Schweitzer." It was the manager of one of the largest stores in Lambaréné. "I have just received a shipment of butter from the Cameroons." Butter had not been available for years. Schweitzer smiled as he entered the store.

At dinner, Schweitzer presented the butter to his hospital staff. Their joy was palpable. Then the doctor grinned and told them the news of the large monetary gift, and everyone's spirit was lightened and lifted in thanks to God.

In the wake of the news, the staff compiled a list of immediate needs. The hospital linen, for instance, was so full of holes that mending it was no longer possible. A second immediate expense was to purchase nearly five thousand pounds of cement to build a landing at the river's edge—a project long overdue.

That letter and the gift were fondly remembered as turning points for the hospital. Schweitzer remained grateful to the Unitarian Service Committee in the United States, which remembered the hospital at a time when no one else did, making it possible for it to continue in operation.

The financial disaster had been averted. Each person's faith had been revived. So had their joy. And so had their commitment to the mission. It was a good day for Lambaréné. And a great day for the kingdom of God.

9

A Lamp Lights the Way

The great secret of success is to go through life as a man who never gets used up.

—ALBERT SCHWEITZER

1945–65

The sound of labored breathing mingles with the swish of the oars slicing through the river's surface. Only a faint crescent of moon is visible among the sparkle of stars that dot the night. The majesty of the sky is unheeded by those in the small canoe.

"Just a little longer," an older woman speaks softly to the woman squatting at her feet.

"We are almost there," a man affirms, pointing to a faint light shining in the distance. A moment later, its reflection glistens on the still water.

"We have reached the landing." The man sighs in relief. "I will find the doctor."

The woman's breathing slows for a moment, and she takes a deep breath, looking up, searching for something to focus on to keep her mind from the intense pain. Her eyes fall on the lamp, around which is inscribed a message: "Here, at whatever hour you come, you will find light and help and human kindness." Another wave of pain washes over her, and she falls to her knees, yet her eyes remain fixed on the lamp.

Help. Help. Human Kindness.

Moments later, voices approach.

"Help her this way," a kind, deep voice speaks with calm authority. A wave of peace washes over the woman, and she knows everything will be okay.

=====

A single ray of light shone through the window as the young woman opened her eyes, focusing on the unfamiliar surroundings.

"Congratulations," a foreign woman spoke as she cradled a baby in her arms. "You have a lovely little girl." She handed the baby to the young woman's mother, who had journeyed with her through the dark night. "I will find the doctor." The nurse took leave.

The young woman took the baby into her arms, gently clasping its tiny hands with her own, mesmerized by the miracle she held.

A shadow appeared in the doorway, and she looked up to see an old man. As he spoke, she recognized the deep, calm voice from the night before.

"That baby of yours gave us a bit of a fight, but everything is fine. You came just in time."

Tears of gratitude welled in the young woman's eyes.

The older woman spoke to the younger: "You were born in this same hospital." Happy wrinkles formed as she smiled at her daughter.

"When I see girls who were born here coming back to the hospital to have babies of their own, that is the only time I know I am growing old."[1] Dr. Schweitzer checked the baby and, after giving her a clean bill of health, left to attend to his other duties.

A nurse gave the young couple the usual instructions provided to first-time parents on the care of newborn babies. Afterward, on their way to the canoe, the young mother and her husband sought out the doctor.

"We wanted to thank you for your help and kindness."

Schweitzer held the tiny baby once more as he answered, "Tell her someday that I was her first admirer. It was here that she had her first night and her first dreams."

———

Over the years, the hospital had expanded to seventy-five buildings. In many ways, it was more of a clinical African community than a pristine European hospital. The buildings sat like barracks, each one stretching from east to west so that the overhanging eaves could provide shade during the hot, muggy days.

Through the center of the village ran a main street, along which the original hospital building had been constructed. The pharmacy complex now served as operating room, sterilizing room, dental clinic, delivery room, nursery, and dressing station. It had sections for a reception room, an examining room, and a dispensary—where patients lined up every morning to have their prescriptions filled.

At the entrance to the hospital, Schweitzer had inscribed in two concrete pillars the ageless promises from Matthew 5: "Blessed are the merciful: for they shall obtain mercy," and

"Blessed are the peacemakers: for they shall be called the children of God."[2]

Behind the main hospital compound stood bungalows where doctors and European patients stayed.

Less than half a mile away, a second group of buildings covered a second hill, reached by a winding path through the foliage. Storerooms, work sheds, nurses' quarters, and wards for female patients and visitors were built there. Farther down the flat-topped hill, closer to the landing, a long, low building housed Dr. Schweitzer, a few staff members, the post office, and the laundry. The hospital kitchen was situated across the way, and next to the kitchen was the staff dining room.

The community facilitated a great variety of needs. There was a urology ward, a home for people suffering from mental disorders, a separate pediatric ward, and another location for obstetric cases. Particular tribes had separate accommodations so as to avoid flare-ups between rival tribes. On average, seven hundred patients received treatment on a daily basis, and each morning, more than a ton of food was provided to the patients and their families.

A path referred to as the Philosophers' Walk[3] branched in another direction through a road dwarfed by overhanging trees and a citrus orchard. At the end of this path, the leper village had been built—fifteen long, low buildings where lepers were treated and housed. Many who suffered from leprosy began treatment only after the disease had affected them in painful ways. Although the disease had ceased its progressive ravaging of their nerves and body tissue, the effects remained obvious. They found themselves on the frayed hem of society;

some refused return by their own villages. Here they found a safe and companionable community where they could not only play a part to keep the village functioning but feel acceptance and love. More than two hundred people made the leper village their home, patients and their children, all of whom performed some form of community service to keep their grounds well tended and running smoothly.

During the day, all manner of animals roamed among the bustling streets of the Schweitzer-Bresslau Hospital. With the family members of patients on their way from one place to another as they cared for their ailing relatives, builders and workmen involved in some construction or reparation project, animals peacefully wandering about, and staff conducting various tasks, the hospital was at times called a place of "orderly confusion."[4]

> The courtyard bordered by the houses of the [foreign] members of the staff is a miniature zoo. Since no animal is wantonly killed near the hospital (the natives finding it more profitable to bring them to Doctor Schweitzer, who always makes a "gift" in return), one never knows what animals will be found there. [In addition to the domestic and farm animals] . . . wild animals are there, too. Under the doctor's house or in pens behind it, there are the antelopes. Monkeys scamper among the trees or on the corrugated roofs. . . . A white owl may be sitting under the piazza roof, or a pelican above the doctor's door, or a stork on the ridge pole. A porcupine may be lumbering around the yard, or a wild pig rooting

about. . . . [A]mong them all the doctor moves, with kindly, observing eye and generous hand, stopping to feed bits of meat to the white owl, or peel an orange for the antelopes, talk to the pelican, or smile at some chimpanzee's comical prank.[5]

As always, Dr. Schweitzer's reverence for life stretched beyond human life, extending to the animal world and beyond. When seeing one of his staff members about to crush a beetle that had been eating through his waterproof jacket, Schweitzer stopped him, saying, "Remember, you are a guest in his country."[6] His daughter, Rhena, remembered that he instructed her never to pluck a flower, which he viewed as an unnecessary destruction of life.

The animals that made their home in the hospital community often had stories of their own, each one having found a kindred spirit and caring friend in Dr. Schweitzer. Leonie, an antelope fawn, was one such creature. As a tiny fawn, it had fallen into a trap with its mother. When the local people arrived, the mother antelope leaped out of the hole and darted away. The fawn was left alone and was taken to the Schweitzer hospital, where the good doctor nursed it from a bottle and kept it in an enclosure near his quarters. In the evenings, it would often be somewhere near Schweitzer as he worked in his study. As it grew older and began developing a taste for his papers, it was allowed to wander the hospital grounds and soon made friends with a couple more antelope fawns named Theodore and Lucie.

Monsieur le Pelican was another creature that found his

home within the welcoming community. He was rescued as a baby, along with two other baby pelicans, and taken to the doctor. Their wings were not developed, so the doctor hand-fed them and kept them under his wide verandah. Eventually they learned to fish on their own, down by the river, and two of them left with the flocks of pelicans at the onset of one wet season. However, Monsieur le Pelican, whose development was always slower than that of the other two, remained behind at the hospital.

"He is my night watchman," Dr. Schweitzer told a visitor one evening as he introduced him to the pelican.

> Every evening at six o'clock, when the bells of the Catholic mission on the island out in the stream begin to toll, he flies up from his fishing down by the river, and takes his place on his perch for the night. And every morning, at six o'clock, when the bells awaken the mission, he spreads his great wings and is off again for his fish. But while he is there during the night, no one can pass up these steps except Mlle. Emma, who has a room in this house, and myself. Everyone else gets a powerful rap on the head. He is a very faithful guardian, and very much of a personality.[7]

Schweitzer's philosophy of reverence for life was apparent in his everyday actions toward every person and creature that came to the banks of his hospital. He treated with concern and dignity all who came to him in need.

Even the animals.

=====

The day begins early in the hospital, sometimes before the sun's rays are sifted by the overhead thatch of leafy branches. Smoke from dozens of cooking stands outside the wards curls upward toward the muted light. Through the morning haze, Le Grand Docteur has already risen to greet the day. He shaves with his old straight-edge razor—no water or soap to assist him.

The morning gong—an unused iron train rail struck by a metal rod—sounds first at six thirty, the hospital's reveille. At seven thirty, it rings once more, signaling breakfast for the hospital staff. In the dining hall, they choose from a variety of jams—made from local fruits—to top their bread, which is baked fresh every day. Coffee and tea are always fresh and strong.

After breakfast, Dr. Schweitzer takes roll outside his quarters. He distributes tools to the laborers—both African and European—and gives them instructions on their tasks for the day. Work begins at eight with another gong of the bell.

At this time patients and their families line up to receive their daily food rations. Afterward, women—wives or daughters of patients—hurry to the water's edge to wash clothes and spread them out on the grass to dry.

Staff members also begin work, which varies, depending on the day of the week and their particular responsibilities. Monday, Wednesday, and Friday are set aside for operations—unless an urgent case shows up unexpectedly. Tuesday, Thursday, and Saturday are given to seeing new patients.

Saturday is also cleaning day and payday. Sunday is a day of rest, meditation, and worship.

On a daily basis, the hospital staff treats patients, changes bandages, and prepares prescriptions. Some staff members devote their time to brighten the days of those suffering from mental illnesses, leading them through simple tasks in the garden or other work that enables them to exercise their abilities and develop self-esteem.

At noon, the bell signals the midday break in work. It sounds again at twelve thirty for lunch. The staff enjoys a meal of salad, bread (with butter twice a week), macaroni, and occasionally a crocodile that had to be shot or some other exotic meat. Again, coffee and tea are always available and plentiful. After half an hour, members of the staff filter off to resume their activities. Sometimes they indulge in a short siesta, recommended by the good doctor, although he rarely takes time for one.

After lunch, the doctor visits the wards or stops by the construction site where a new surgical ward is under way. Sometimes he can be seen hunched over his desk, answering the ever-present bulk of mail. At two, the bell gongs once again, and patients line up outside the dispensary for their daily prescribed medication. The medicine is taken on the spot so that nurses can ensure it is not forgotten, thrown away, or strung on a necklace as a charm.

When shadows begin to fall across the buildings, one more bell sounds at five thirty to mark the end of the workday. Because electricity is not available in the hospital—except for a small generator used to power the x-ray machine and lights in the case of emergency nighttime surgery—each staff member has a kerosene lamp, carrying it as they complete their duties for the evening and make their way to the hall for dinner at seven o'clock.

They turn down their lamps and place them along the dining room entrance before seating themselves inside. The white tablecloth reflects a soft glow from the shining lanterns as a short prayer by Dr. Schweitzer signals the beginning of the meal. Hushed, but friendly, conversation ensues around a meal of soup, vegetables, and fish. Sometimes Schweitzer notices that someone looks a little hungrier than usual, or perhaps he remembers that a particular dish is the person's favorite. He passes half his serving of fish or a dish of pineapple toward the person with a simple, "Here, that is for you."[8] Coffee and cake often follow the main course.

Once all have eaten, the plates are traded for hymnbooks. Dr. Schweitzer gives the page number as he makes his way to the piano, which is set against the wall, between two large windows. Although the same hymns are frequently repeated, his prelude to each is always original—played with a classical touch one day and given another unique style the next. The hymn is always over too soon to fully enjoy such brilliant improvisation. The piano is no longer tuned to perfection, nor can it be due to decades of deterioration in the topical climate.

Schweitzer returns to his place and begins to read the Bible verses he has selected, followed by the Lord's Prayer. He reads in German, and a short, but interesting discussion or commentary ensues. He often follows the reading in French if there are those who do not speak German. The resultant discourse is more often than not interrupted by the faithful cuckoo clock sounding out the hour.

After a few more moments, the doctor remarks, "Fine, and now back to work."[9] Before departing, he often adds, "My door is open." Staff members are free to come to their resident father figure with concerns or problems, sure to be met with trust and compassion. Visitors often have questions or request interviews, which he always accommodates.

Staff members usually continue their conversations after dinner. They discuss events of the day, highlights in the news, or changes in the weather. Sometimes a record is played on the phonograph. The constant background music is, as always, the sounds of the African forest at night—bullfrogs, cicadas, and the gentle rustling of the towering palms. After an eventful day, it is not long before conversation quiets, and once more, lanterns light up the walk back down the path toward the staff quarters. The final bell sounds for curfew at nine o'clock.

At times, the gentle notes of Bach are heard drifting from Schweitzer's room, where he still uses the piano constructed with foot pedals for organ practice. Other times, he sits at his desk well into the night, painstakingly composing a letter or a note of thanks in spite of the persistent cramp in his writing hand.

From the 1950s onward, a capable staff took care of the daily tasks and operations. They met together regularly to vote on policy or other pertinent matters. Dr. Schweitzer, of course, offered counsel and insight from his vast experience and excellent recall of past surgeries and the numerous medical cases he treated through the years. A skilled surgeon,

Rolf Müller, served as his chief of staff from 1959 until 1964. Although Albert Schweitzer did not perform surgeries during the last fifteen years of his life, the Lambaréné staff depended on his wisdom. He remained fully occupied with the oversight of many aspects of the hospital's inner workings.

Some individuals during the later period of Schweitzer's life criticized the old-fashioned modes of operation in the hospital community, suggesting that the doctor embrace large-scale public health projects and research projects. His reply was simply that he was too old and that those who followed must be the ones to take up the torch of change and modernization.[10]

In the early years of service, when Schweitzer first came to Africa, he was the only doctor within a thousand-mile radius. In his later years, however, medical personnel from countries worldwide offered their skills to the hospital, which by then was well-known as a major medical institution. Schweitzer often remembered the days when he had only two helpers— his wife and Nurse Kottmann—for the better part of 1946.

In 1947, Hélène's health deteriorated so much she needed to return to Switzerland. Albert remained in Africa for another year. It was the longest period of time he had spent in Africa, with only a twelve-day stay in Europe before the war had begun. By October 1948, enough volunteers had come to Lambaréné to staff the hospital, making it possible for him to return to Europe.

He reunited with his wife and daughter once more and

met his four grandchildren for the first time. His daughter, Rhena, had married an engineer and organ builder, Jean Eckert, in 1939. They settled in Switzerland, near Zürich, where all their children were educated.

Schweitzer made his first and only trip to the United States in July 1949. The University of Chicago and the Ford Foundation invited him to speak on the occasion of the Goethe Bicentennial Assembly held in Aspen, Colorado. With the funds received during his short stay in the United States, Schweitzer could afford to renovate the hospital grounds.

That October, he returned to Africa for his eighth sojourn. He remained for twenty months and directed the rebuilding of the hospital, which had suffered from disrepair during the financial shortage of the war years.

Throughout the 1950s, as during a period twenty years earlier, Dr. Schweitzer traveled fairly often between Gabon and Europe. He made five visits to Europe in that decade, each tour lasting around six months. As before, he gave speeches and received invitations to many places throughout Europe. He always accepted invitations to speak to school-children, believing that the future of philosophy was held in the hearts of the youth.[11]

His work became more widely known during this period, and he received numerous awards and honors. In 1951, his promotion of world peace earned a prize of ten thousand marks from the West German Association of Book Publishers and Sellers. In 1952, his humanitarian efforts earned him the Prince Carl Medal, awarded by King Gustav Adolf of Sweden. In 1953, while he was busy at work in Africa, his continuing efforts and achievements earned him the ultimate tribute of the Nobel Peace Prize. Because he was not in Europe to receive the honor, the French ambassador accepted the prize on his behalf. Dr. Schweitzer used the award money to finance the building of the leper village in Lambaréné. The following year, in November, Schweitzer delivered his Nobel Peace Prize acceptance speech titled "The Problem of Peace in the World Today":

> Today . . . we live in a period that is marked by the absence of peace; today . . . nations feel themselves menaced by other nations. . . .
>
> May those who have in their hands the fate of the nations . . . take to heart the words of the Apostle Paul: "If it be possible, as much as lieth in you, live peaceably with all men." His words are valid not only for individuals, but for whole nations as well. May the nations, in their efforts to keep peace in being, go to the farthest limits of possibility, so that the spirit of man shall be given time to develop and grow strong—and time to act.[12]

Schweitzer was also welcomed into the French Academy of Moral and Political Sciences in 1952 and accepted into the American Academy of Arts and Sciences in absentia.[13]

Now approaching eighty years of age, he began to speak out against the dangers of the nuclear age. His stance was that in the event of a nuclear war, there would be no winners. All would lose through the wanton and widespread destruction of life.

In autumn of 1956, Hélène joined her husband a final time in Africa. She remained there until March 1957 when her ailing health sent her back to Switzerland. She passed away on May 30, 1957. Albert arrived by boat three weeks later and remained in Switzerland until the end of the year. Upon his return to Africa, he carried her ashes with him and buried her beneath a small cross that he carved. The cross stood outside his window, and next to it, a second cross marked the grave of the dedicated nurse Mademoiselle Emma Hausknecht, who had died in Lambaréné the previous year.

The passing of many of his friends and loved ones brought the realization to Schweitzer that his time of departure would likewise come. Yet he refused to be intimidated by the prospect of death. He said,

> Only familiarity with the thought of death creates true, inward freedom from material things. The ambition, greed, and love of power that we keep in our hearts, that shackle us to this life in chains of bondage, cannot in the long run deceive the man who looks death in the face. Rather, by contemplating his end, he eventually feels purified and delivered from his baser self, from material things, and from other men, as well as from fear and hatred of his fellow men.[14]

In 1958, Albert Schweitzer made a trip to Europe. He closed down the house in Switzerland and returned his belongings to his father's vicarage in Günsbach, where he grew up. He recalled with fondness his father's sermons, which made a great impression on his life. Schweitzer knew that his father's sermons were an honest part of his own life and experiences as he opened his heart and life to his parish time and again. As a child, though, Schweitzer's favorite services were on Sunday afternoons. The first Sunday of each month, his father spoke of the life and work of missionaries and created in Albert's heart from a young age admiration for missionaries and interest in mission work. He remembered the many Sundays that his father read the memoirs of Mr. Casalis—missionary to South Africa—which he had translated into French so he could read them to his church.[15]

During that trip to Europe, he delivered three lectures, "Peace or Atomic War," which aired three times in early 1958 on Radio Oslo (Norway):

> The awareness that we are all human beings together has become lost in war and politics. We have reached the point of regarding each other only as members of a people either allied with us or against us and our approach: prejudice, sympathy, or antipathy are all conditioned by that. . . .
>
> At the present time when violence, clothed in life, dominates the world more cruelly than it ever has before, I still remain convinced that truth, love, peaceableness, meekness, and kindness are the violence which can master all other violence. . . .
>
> In the hearts of people today there is a deep longing for peace. When the true spirit of peace is thoroughly dominant, it becomes an inner experience with unlimited possibilities. It is only when this really happens, that

the spirit of peace awakens and takes possession of men's hearts, that humanity can be saved from perishing.[16]

While he was there, he was awarded the Sonning Prize, granting him ten thousand Danish crowns, as well as the Joseph Lemaire Prize. Schweitzer returned to Africa later that year, never to return to Europe. Once he was heard to say that the Africans were his people, and they would not understand if he left and died on "foreign" soil.[17]

Upon his return, Schweitzer wrote to his daughter, asking if she would be interested in traveling to Lambaréné to celebrate their joint birthday together. She agreed and thus began a new phase in her life. Rhena enjoyed her time in Lambaréné so immensely that she vowed to return that she might devote, as her father had, her efforts to the people of Gabon. Once her children were all away at school, she studied and received certification as a laboratory technician, returning often to Lambaréné to offer her services to her father, which he gladly accepted.

It was 1965, Schweitzer's final year in this world. Though his time was short, the deepest concerns of his heart still rested with the people of the world, especially those who bore what he called "the Mark of Pain."[18]

In April, he spoke to a fellow doctor, Joseph Franklin Montague, who later wrote a book titled *The Why of Albert Schweitzer*. In it Montague recalls Schweitzer's words:

I have been privileged, to have been physician for count-less of my fellow men, those who suffered greatly as they crawled along jungle trails, or paddled their pirogues through the river in search of help during their hour of great need. There is an inner glow, a deep satisfaction every time I am blessed to bring surcease from pain, to turn dying hope into concrete help and revive a weary or sick individual.

There have been countless advances in the medi-cal field, from the time I began my practice until now. Doctors today are blessed to have much in their medical arsenal with which they can relieve the pain and heal the afflictions of the sick. Yet, in the midst of these wondrous discoveries, I am saddened to notice a decline in empathy of physicians towards patients. The patient is not merely another case, but is a fellow human being; and I have seen the same lack of regard in patients for their doctors. Beyond that, how many generations not yet born will suf-fer from the present race toward nuclear capabilities?[19]

A few months later, although suffering from deep fatigue, Schweitzer confided in his daughter that perhaps he could prepare one last appeal for peace: "Perhaps I should make another world-wide radio appeal, like I did in Oslo. If only I can have the time, and am not too tired . . . I should make one more effort."[20]

10

A Good Shepherd's Testimony

As we acquire more knowledge, things do not become more comprehensible but more mysterious.

—ALBERT SCHWEITZERS

September 4, 1965

Albert Schweitzer, at ninety years old, suffered from fatigue during the hot summer months. In spite of that, on August 12, a surge of energy arose in him as he heard the chanting song of rowers announcing the arrival of friends. Schweitzer walked to the landing to greet the small group from Switzerland and Alsace.

The members of the Association of the Albert Schweitzer Hospital had undertaken the responsibility of continuing the hospital in the event that Dr. Schweitzer would no longer be able to.

August 23 was the last day that the doctor took his usual place at the dinner table. Afterward, he followed the comfortable tradition of reading from the Bible and playing a hymn. However, he departed from the usual discussion on the Bible reading and instead returned to his seat, saying, "I wish to review my hopes for the continuation of the hospital and share my requests for its maintenance in the event of my passing."[1]

Fritz Dinner, a member of the Association of the Albert Schweitzer Hospital who had arrived on the twelfth, was impressed by the calm, yet clear manner in which Dr. Schweitzer relayed his instructions. After the short discussion, fatigue took over, and the aging doctor retired to his room.

A couple of days after the evening discussion, Schweitzer requested to be driven around the grounds in the hospital's jeep. Fritz Dinner remarked at the sight: "One could observe that his eyes wandered over the hospital and its buildings as if he took them in, like the last view of his life's work, or—who can tell—as though taking leave."[2]

Albert Schweitzer spent the next week in bed, cared for by his daughter and members of the staff—those who, if not for his example of dedication and mercy, would have found their lives following a much different path.

On August 28, as his daughter sat by his bedside, he spoke to her in a tired voice: "Rhena, I see that you love the people here."

"Yes, Father, as you have loved them with all your heart." She took his hand in hers.

"Will you stay as administrator? They need someone with a strong spirit, a sharp mind, and a soft heart." His voice was soft, almost pleading.

"I will stay. The work will continue. Don't worry. We will not let the memory fade."

His eyelids closed for a few moments, and she thought he was asleep when they fluttered open again. "There is still much work to be done."

On September 4, 1965, at 10:30 p.m., Albert Schweitzer quietly slipped away from the life to which he had clung tenaciously for so many years—not for his sake, but for the sake of others in need.

Joseph F. Montague wrote that if a list were to be made of his possessions at the end of his life, it would include:

One pith helmet
One old felt hat (soiled)
Six short-sleeved white shirts
One bow tie (ready made)
Six pairs of white slacks
One pair of shoes; accessory socks and underwear
One old-fashioned straight razor
and *the good will of more than half of the world!*[4]

Many who had known Albert Schweitzer during his life wrote of him after his death, painting a clear picture of a man whose ethics, empathy, and dedication set him apart from the average life. As Albert Einstein, who preceded Schweitzer in death, once said of him, "Here in this sorry world is a *man!*"[4]

Einstein wrote,

I have scarcely ever known personally a single individual in whom goodness and the need for beauty are merged to such a degree of unity as in the case of Albert Schweitzer. . . .

Everywhere he avoided rigid tradition. He fights against it anywhere it is in any way hopeful for the individual. . . .

He did not preach and did not warn and did not dream that his example would be an ideal and a comfort to innumerable people. He simply acted out of inner necessity.[5]

In *Schweitzer: A Biography*, the authors observed that Albert Schweitzer "was a man torn between two countries and then later two continents, who in the end rose above geographical confinement in his emergence as a world citizen. . . . [H]e refused to be bound by nationalism or narrow loyalty. His was a total commitment to all humanity and to a universal culture and ethic he wished for all the world."[6]

As for his own perception of his work, when asked about his major life's accomplishments and how he would like to be identified, he replied, "As a philosopher."

"But what about your music?"

With his trademark smile, he responded, "That's my hobby."[7]

═══

Months after the death of Le Grand Docteur, individuals still made their way to his grave site on Sunday afternoons, weaving up the hill from the landing, glowing candles marking their pilgrimage. At his grave, groups of up to one hundred people stood and read verses from the Bible, prayed, and spoke. Some laid down bouquets of flowers. Others offered presents to the hospital staff, gifts from the depths of their hearts. As evening fell, they retreated up the hill, donned tribal masks, and danced to the dull beat of the village drums.

"What is it that they say?" asked a volunteer at the hospital one day.

An older African translated words that were spoken from the heart of each one touched by the service of a single, ordinary, yet uncommon life: "We thank God that he sent Dr. Schweitzer to us and that he was our good shepherd who gave his life for us, stayed with us, was buried in our soil and under our palm trees."[8]

And somewhere, beyond the distant stars, yet closer than the silent breath of the wind, a soul who had made his life his greatest testimony rested in eternal peace and delighted in the unsurpassed joy of his Lord.

Afterword

If only the idea of reverence for life and the true spirit of Christianity could be merged into one great philosophy, an ethic so simple that everybody could understand it. . . . It would give birth to a new attitude, and my life's work would not have been in vain. Then this world could become a better place to live in.

—ALBERT SCHWEITZER

The Mysterious Ripple Effect

In *Memoirs of Childhood and Youth*, Albert Schweitzer wrote of the often unknown effect that one individual has upon another:

> So many people gave me something or were something to me without knowing it. . . . Much that has become our own in gentleness, modesty, kindness, willingness to forgive, in veracity, loyalty, resignation under suffering, we owe to people in whom we have seen or experienced these virtues at work. . . . A thought which had become act sprang into us like a spark, and lighted a new flame within us.
>
> . . . [O]ur own light goes out, and is rekindled by some experience we go through with a fellow-man. Thus we have each of us cause to think with deep gratitude of those who have lighted the flames within us. . . .
>
> Similarly, not one of us knows what effect his life produces, and what he gives to others; that is hidden from us and must remain so, though we are often allowed to see some little fraction of it so that we may not lose courage. The way in which this power works is a mystery.[1]

It is, indeed, a mystery. To accurately document the lasting effects produced in the world through Albert Schweitzer's life and testimony would be similar to following the life of a drop of water through its phases of water, vapor, and ice and determining its effects in nature.

There are the thousands who found relief and healing through the treatments during the fifty-two years that Dr. Schweitzer worked in Lambaréné.

There are the millions who heard about and read of his life and work, none of whom could remain completely untouched by the toss of the single stone into the lake of humanity, sending ripples through its collective soul. "There is no limit to the effects that one dedicated person can make in the lives of those in need."

How far have those ripples traveled? Beyond the soul? Indeed. Beyond borders? Definitely. Beyond boulders? Emphatically, as stated in Beyond Boulders: Blog of the Albert Schweitzer Fellowship (ASF):

> In his autobiography, Out of My Life and Thought, Nobel Peace Laureate (and ASF namesake) Dr. Albert Schweitzer described the necessary obstacles and challenges we all must overcome as "boulders," noting, "Anyone who proposes to do good must not expect people to roll stones out of his way, but must accept his lot calmly if they even roll a few more upon it. A strength which becomes clearer and stronger through its experience of such obstacles is the only strength that can conquer them."
>
> Here at ASF, we support Schweitzer Fellows in

discovering and developing that strength as they conceptualize and carry out yearlong service projects that address unmet health needs—and develop into lifelong Leaders in Service in the process. This blog chronicles their journey of moving beyond the boulders they encounter.[2]

It is apparent by this blog that the ripple effect continues. The Albert Schweitzer Fellowship states that its mission is to "develop 'leaders in service': individuals who are dedicated and skilled in addressing the health needs of underserved communities, and whose example influences and inspires others."[3]

One example of the work of ASF is this program in the Albert Schweitzer Hospital: "In 1999, The Albert Schweitzer Fellowship helped establish the Community Health Program, which provides comprehensive village-based healthcare, vaccinations, and health education. With active support from the Ministry of Health, UNICEF, and the U.S. Peace Corps, this program serves as a national model. Efforts are underway to expand the program to include prevention and treatment programs for HIV/AIDS, TB, and other diseases."[4]

And what of the Schweitzer Hospital? Has it faded into the background, disappearing back into the steamy jungle overgrowth of West Gabon? Hardly. It is still supported by Schweitzer organizations worldwide as well as by the Gabonese government. The hospital still has a homey village feel, all the while keeping pace with the ever-evolving needs of a changing world:

Today, an international staff of Gabonese and expatriate professionals provide skilled care for over 35,000 outpatient visits and more than 6,000 hospitalizations annually for patients from all parts of Gabon. Two surgeons and their teams carry out close to 2,200 operations annually. Most of the 160 members of the staff live in the hospital compound, which gives the hospital the feel of a village.

Through support from the Gabonese government and Schweitzer organizations around the world, patients today find a modern medical facility that includes two operating rooms, a dental clinic, and inpatient wards for pediatric, adult medicine, surgical, and obstetrical patients.

The U.S. National Institute of Health has recognized the Hospital's research laboratory as one of five leading facilities in Africa engaged in scientific studies of malaria, the greatest killer on the African continent with more than 1,000,000 deaths per year. Children with severe malaria at the Schweitzer Hospital have the lowest documented mortality rate anywhere on the continent. . . .

In 2008 the Albert Schweitzer Hospital initiated a strategic planning process to guide the growth of the hospital over the next three to five years, leading up to the celebration in 2013 of the Hospital's 100th anniversary. This "Lambaréné Centennial Project" aims at strengthening clinical and public health programs in HIV/AIDS, TB, malaria, and maternal/child health so that the Schweitzer Hospital is a model of integrated hospital and village health programs in rural Africa, and a training site for health workers from throughout the region.[5]

From that single stone—an individual willing to lose himself along the shores of an unknown village a century ago—the ripples will continue to spread outward and touch upon the shores of mankind.

Montague wrote of Schweitzer, "As a spiritual force he still lives on. The example of his great character, the tenets of his philosophy, and the effects of his good work continue to exert their beneficial influence in the world of thinking people. It will continue to do so as long as sincerity, honesty of intent, and courage to face reality exist in the human mind."[6]

Albert Schweitzer understood the significance of service, the lasting legacy of love, and the power of a promise given two thousand years ago: "Whosoever will come after me, let him deny himself, and take up his cross, and follow me. For whosoever will save his life shall lose it; but whosoever shall lose his life for my sake and the gospel's, the same shall save it" (Mark 8:34–35).

Acknowledgment

I would like to acknowledge my indebtedness to Bonita Jewel for her help with this manuscript.

Without her tireless work, her enthusiastic attitude, and her amazing gifts, this book would not have been possible.

Appendix 1

Quotes from Albert Schweitzer

Gratitude

"We ought all to make an effort to act on our first thoughts and let our unspoken gratitude find expression. Then there will be more sunshine in the world, and more power to work for what is good. . . . A great deal of water is flowing underground which never comes up as a spring. In that thought we may find comfort. But we ourselves must try to be the water which does find its way up; we must become a spring at which men can quench their thirst for gratitude."[1]

The Kingdom of God

"The miracle must happen in us before it can happen in the world. We dare not set our hope on our own efforts to create the conditions for God's Kingdom in the world. We must indeed labor for its realization. But there can be no Kingdom of God in the world without the Kingdom of God in our hearts. The starting point is our determined effort to bring every thought and action under the sway of the Kingdom of God. Nothing can be achieved without inwardness. The Spirit of God will only strive against the spirit of the world when it has won its victory over that spirit in our hearts."[2]

The Interconnectedness of All Life

"The deeper we look into nature, the more we recognize that it is full of life, and the more profoundly we know that all life is a secret and that we are united with all life that is in nature. Man can no longer live his life for himself alone. We realize that all life is valuable and that we are united to all this life. From this knowledge comes our spiritual relationship to the universe."[3]

Reverence for Life

"The fundamental fact of human awareness is this: 'I am life that wants to live in the midst of other life that wants to live.' A thinking man feels compelled to approach all life with the same reverence he has for his own. Thus, all life becomes part of his own experience. From such a point of view, 'good' means to maintain life, to further life, to bring developing life to its highest level. 'Evil' means to destroy life, to hurt life, to keep life from developing. This, then, is the rational, universal, and basic principle of ethics."[4]

"Just as white light consists of colored rays, so reverence for life contains all the components of ethics: love, kindliness, sympathy, empathy, peacefulness, power to forgive."[5]

Knowledge

"The highest knowledge is to know that we are surrounded by mystery."[6]

Jesus as Lord

"Christianity is a Christ-Mysticism, that is to say, a 'belonging together' with Christ as our Lord, grasped in thought and realised in experience. By simply designating Jesus 'our Lord' Paul raises Him above all the temporally conditioned conceptions in which the mystery of His personality might be grasped, and sets Him forth as the spiritual Being who transcends all human definitions, to whom we have to surrender ourselves in order to experience in Him the true law of our existence and our being."[7]

Religion Does Not Explain Everything

"When you preach the Gospel, beware of preaching it as

the religion which explains everything. I suppose that in England, as on the Continent, thousands and thousands of men have despaired of Christianity, because they have seen and experienced the atrocities of the War. Confronted with the inexplicable, the religion which they believed to have an explanation for everything has collapsed.

"For ten years, before I left for Africa, I prepared boys in the parish of St. Nicholas, in Strassburg, for confirmation. After the War some of them came to see me and thanked me for having taught them so definitely that religion was not a formula for explaining everything. They said it had been that teaching which had kept them from discarding Christianity, whereas so many others in the trenches discarded it, not being prepared to meet the inexplicable."[8]

Union with God

"When you preach, you must lead men out of the desire to know everything to the knowledge of the one thing that is needful, to desire to be in God, and thus no more to conform to the world but to rise above all mysteries as those who are redeemed from the world. 'If only I have Thee, I care nothing for heaven and earth.' 'All things work together for good to them that love God.' Point men to these words as to the peaks of Ararat, where they may take refuge when the flood of the inexplicable overwhelms all around."[9]

"God's love speaks to us in our hearts and tries to work through us in the world. We must listen to it as to a pure and distant melody that comes across the noise of the world's doings. Some say, 'When we are grown up, we would rather think of other things.' But the voice of Love with which God speaks to us in the secret places of the heart, speaks to us when we are young so that our youth may be really youth, and that we may become the children of God. Happy are those who listen."[10]

The Little Task

"Always keep your eyes open for the little task, because it is the little task that is important to Jesus Christ. The future of the Kingdom of God does not depend on the enthusiasm of this or that powerful person; those great ones are necessary too, but it is equally necessary to have a great number of little people who will do a little thing in the service of Christ.

"The great flowing rivers represent only a small part of all the water that is necessary to nourish and sustain the earth. Beside the flowing river there is the water in the earth—the subterranean water—and there are the little streams which continually enter the river and feed it and prevent it from sinking into the earth. Without these other waters—the silent hidden subterranean waters and the trickling streams—the great river could no longer flow. Thus it is with the little tasks to be fulfilled by us all."[11]

Appendix 2

Bibliography of Albert Schweitzer's Books

1. Autobiography

African Notebook. Trans. Mrs. C. E. B. Russell. New York: Henry Holt, 1939.

Afrikanische Jagdgeschichten. Strasbourg: Editions des Sources, 1936. Translated in *The Animal World of Albert Schweitzer.* (See below under Collections and Compilations.)

Das Spital im Urwald. Bern: Paul Haupt, 1948. Partially translated in *The Animal World of Albert Schweitzer.* (See below under Collections and Compilations.)

Eight Years in Lambaréné Hospital from 1946 to 1954. New York: Albert Schweitzer Fellowship, 1955, 22 pages.

The Hospital at Lambaréné During the War Years, 1939–1945. New York: Albert Schweitzer Fellowship, 1947, 19 pages.

Memoirs of Childhood and Youth. trans. C. T. Campion. New York: Macmillan, 1931.

Mitteilungen aus Lambaréné. Three booklets.

   1—1924. Bern: Paul Haupt, 1925.
   2—1924–25. Bern: Paul Haupt, 1926.
   3—1925–27. Bern: Paul Haupt, 1928.

On the Edge of the Primeval Forest and *The Forest Hospital at Lambaréné.* Both trans. C. T. Campion. Combined in one volume. New York: Macmillan, 1948.

Out of My Life and Thought. trans. C. T. Campion. New York: Henry Holt, 1948.

Selbstdarstellung. In vol. 7 of *Die Philosophie der Gegenwart in Selbstdarstellungen,* edited by Dr. Raymund Schmidt. Leipzig: Felix Meiner, 1929.

2. Biography

"My First Organ Teacher: Eugène Munch, 1857–1898." In *Music in the Life of Albert Schweitzer,* 9–24. (See below under Collections and Compilations.)

Goethe: Four Studies. Trans. Charles R. Joy. Boston: Beacon Press, 1949.

3. Religion and Theology

Das Abendmahl im Zusammenhang mit dem Leben Jesu und der Geschichte des Urchristentums. Vol. 1. Das Abendmahlsproblem auf Grund der wissenschaftlichen Forschung des 19. Jahrhunderts und der historischen Berichte. Tübingen: J. C. B. Mohr (Paul Siebeck), 1901. Vol. 2 has been translated under the title *The Mystery of the Kingdom of God.* (See below.)

Christianity and the Religions of the World. Trans. Joanna Powers. New York: Henry Holt, 1939.

Kingdom of God and Primitive Christianity. New York: Seabury Press, 1966.

The Mystery of the Kingdom of God. Trans. Walter Lowrie. New York: Dodd, Mead, 1914.

The Mysticism of Paul the Apostle. Trans. W. Montgomery. New York: Henry Holt, 1931.

Paul and His Interpreters. Trans. W. Montgomery. New York: Macmillan, 1912.

The Quest of the Historical Jesus: A Critical Study of Its Progress from Reimarus to Wrede. Trans. W. Montgomery. New York: Macmillan, 1945.

4. Philosophy and Ethics

Civilization and Ethics. Being part 2 of *The Philosophy of Civilization.* trans. C. T. Campion. New York: Macmillan, 1929.

The Decay and Restoration of Civilization. Being part 1 of *The Philosophy of Civilization.* trans. C. T. Campion. New York: Macmillan, 1932.

Indian Thought and Its Development. Trans. Mrs. C. E. B. Russell. New York: Henry Holt, 1936.

Peace or Atomic War? New York: Holt, 1961.

Die Religionsphilosophie Kants von der "Kritik der reinen Vernunft" bis zur "Religion innerhalb der Grenzen der blossen Vernunft." Tübingen: J. C. B. Mohr (Paul Siebeck), 1899.

Reverence for Life. New York: Harper & Row, 1969.

5. Psychiatry

The Psychiatric Study of Jesus. Trans. Charles R. Joy. Boston: Beacon Press, 1948.

6. Music

"The Art of Organ Building and Organ Playing in Germany and France." In *Music in the Life of Albert Schweitzer*, 138–76. (See below under Collections and Compilations.)

Johann Sebastian Bach. Trans. Ernest Newman. 2 vols. London: A. & C. Black, 1938.

Johann Sebastian Bach: Complete Organ Works. Copyright renewed, 1940. New York: G. Schirmer, 1911. Originally published in 5 vols. in German.

J. S. Bach, le Musicien-Poète. Leipzig: Breitkopf und Härtel, 1905. Translated in part in *Music in the Life of Albert Schweitzer*, 68–135. (See below under Collections and Compilations.)

J. S. Bachs Präludien und Fugen für Orgel, kritische Ausgabe mit praktischen Angaben über die Wiedergabe dieser Werke. 5 vols.. New York: Schirmer, 1911.

Règles internationals pour la Construction des Orges. Internationales Regulativ für Orgelbau. In collaboration with the Abbé X. Mathias. Vienna: Artaria, 1909.

═══

Collections and Compilations Based on Albert Schweitzer's Writings

Albert Schweitzer: An Anthology. Edited by Charles Joy. Boston: Beacon Press, 1947.

The Animal World of Albert Schweitzer. Translated and edited by Charles R. Joy. Boston: Beacon Press, 1950.

Goethe: Five Studies. Edited by Charles Joy and Albert Schweitzer. Boston: Beacon Press, 1961.

Music in the Life of Albert Schweitzer. Edited by Charles Joy. New York: Harper & Bros., 1951.

Pilgrimage to Humanity. Edited by Albert Schweitzer. New York: Philosophical Library, 1961.

Appendix 3

The Hospital Today

Objectives of the Albert Schweitzer Hospital

+ Translate the Charter of Values into action in the hospital.
+ Involve the Albert Schweitzer Hospital in the health policy of Gabon and surrounding countries.
+ Identify the medical and socio-medical needs on preventive and curative bases; formulate solutions in a flexible community health framework in an effort to become a model for health care in Africa.
+ Become a site of clinical research.
+ Become a site of training
    For Gabonese medical and non-medical personnel
    For foreign medical and non-medical personnel
+ To promote health education for the population, encouraging the community's own local health education initiatives
+ Manage and organize the site and all the work of

the Albert Schweitzer Hospital by ensuring the protection of ecosystems as Schweitzer did.

+ Create a venue for international interaction, dialogue and mutual enrichment, combining thought and action in medical, ethical, philosophical, artistic, cultural and pedagogical arenas.[1]

Notes

Chapter 1: The Tolling of the Bell at Lambaréné

1. George Marshall and David Poling, *Schweitzer: A Biography* (Garden City, NY: Doubleday, 1971), prologue.
2. Ibid., 306–7.
3. Ibid., 307.

Chapter 2: First Glimpses of a Foreign Shore

1. Albert Schweitzer, *Memoirs of Childhood and Youth*, trans. C. T. Campion (New York: Macmillan, 1958), 28–29.
2. Ibid., 28.
3. Albert Schweitzer, *On the Edge of the Primeval Forest* and *More from the Primeval Forest*, trans. C. T. Campion (New York: Macmillan, 1948), 1.
4. Albert Schweitzer, *Out of My Life and Thought: An Autobiography*, trans. C. T. Campion (New York: Henry Holt, 1933), 106–7.
5. Ibid., 73–75.

Chapter 3: A Home Among the Hills

1. Albert Schweitzer, *On the Edge of the Primeval Forest* and *More from the Primeval Forest*, trans. C. T. Campion (New York: Macmillan, 1948), 24.
2. Ibid., 20.
3. Ibid., 22.

4. Ibid.

5. Ibid., 25.

6. Ibid., 78.

7. George Marshall, and David Poling, *Schweitzer: A Biography* (Garden City, NY: Doubleday, 1971), 115.

8. Albert Schweitzer, *Out of My Life and Thought: An Autobiography*, trans. C. T. Campion (New York: Henry Holt, 1933), 170.

Chapter 4: The Peaceful Prisoner of War

1. Albert Schweitzer, *Out of My Life and Thought: An Autobiography*, trans. C. T. Campion (New York: Henry Holt, 1933), 172–73.

2. Ibid., 174.

3. Ibid.

4. Ibid., 175.

5. Albert Schweitzer, *On the Edge of the Primeval Forest* and *More from the Primeval Forest*, trans. C. T. Campion (New York: Macmillan, 1948), 93.

6. Ibid.

7. Ibid., 92.

8. George Marshall and David Poling, *Schweitzer: A Biography* (Garden City, NY: Doubleday, 1971), 137.

9. Schweitzer, *Out of My Life and Thought*, 185–86.

10. Ibid., 188–89.

11. Marshall and Poling, *Schweitzer: A Biography*, 143.

12. Schweitzer, *On the Edge of the Primeval Forest*, 96.

13. Ibid.

14. Ibid., 99.

15. Schweitzer, *Out of My Life and Thought*, 191.

16. Ibid., 194.

17. Ibid., 195.

18. Ibid., 198.

19. Albert Schweitzer, *Memoirs of Childhood and Youth*, trans. C. T. Campion (New York: Macmillan, 1958), 40.

20. Ibid., 40–41.

21. Ibid.

22. Ibid., 41.

23. Schweitzer, *Out of My Life and Thought*, 202.

Chapter 5: Three Sacrifices Returned

1. Henry Clark, *The Ethical Mysticism of Albert Schweitzer* (Boston: Beacon Press, 1962), 51.

2. Erica Anderson, *The Schweitzer Album* (New York: Harper & Row, 1965), 20.

3. Albert Schweitzer, *Out of My Life and Thought: An Autobiography*, trans. C. T. Campion (New York: Henry Holt, 1933), 217.

4. Ibid., 218.

5. Ibid., 229.

6. Albert Schweitzer, *Memoirs of Childhood and Youth*, trans. C. T. Campion (New York: Macmillan, 1958), 76.

7. Ibid., 77.

8. Ibid., 77–78.

Chapter 6: Living in Lambaréné

1. Albert Schweitzer, *On the Edge of the Primeval Forest and More from the Primeval Forest*, trans. C. T. Campion (New York: Macmillan, 1948), 123.

2. Ibid., 124.

3. Ibid., 125.

4. Ibid., 126.

5. Ibid., 129.

6. Ibid., 134–35.

7. Manioc, also known as cassava, grew as a root up to three feet long and six to nine inches in diameter. The root was filled with a milky substance. One variety of manioc contains cyanic acid, deadly to ingest. In order to render the root edible, people soaked it in running water for days. Afterward, they crushed the root and worked it into a dark, thick dough upon fermentation. Then they worked it into sticks and wrapped it in leaves to keep fresh.

8. Schweitzer, *On the Edge of the Primeval Forest and More from the Primeval Forest*, 145.

9. Ibid., 146.
10. George Marshall and David Poling, *Schweitzer: A Biography* (Garden City, NY: Doubleday, 1971), 167.
11. Schweitzer, *On the Edge of the Primeval Forest*, 218.

Chapter 7: Living Between Two Worlds

1. Albert Schweitzer, *Out of My Life and Thought: An Autobiography*, trans. C. T. Campion (New York: Henry Holt, 1933), 242–43.
2. Joseph Franklin Montague, *The Why of Albert Schweitzer* (New York: Hawthorn, 1965), 9.
3. George Marshall and David Poling, *Schweitzer: A Biography* (Garden City, NY: Doubleday, 1971), 195–96.
4. Ibid., 189.
5. Hans Walter Bahr, ed., *Albert Schweitzer Letters, 1905–1965*, trans. Joachim Neugroschel (New York: Macmillan, 1992), 158–59.

Chapter 8: Little Miracles in Lambaréné

1. George Marshall and David Poling, *Schweitzer: A Biography* (Garden City, NY: Doubleday, 1971), 213.
2. Hans Walter Bahr, ed., *Albert Schweitzer Letters, 1905–1965*, trans. Joachim Neugroschel (New York: Macmillan, 1992), 172. The letter was postmarked 25 October 1943.
3. Ibid., 176–77.
4. Marshall and Poling, *Schweitzer: A Biography*, 216.
5. Ibid, 218.

Chapter 9: A Lamp Lights the Way

1. Erica Anderson, *The Schweitzer Album* (New York: Harper & Row, 1965), 64.
2. Ibid., 55.
3. Joseph Franklin Montague, *The Why of Albert Schweitzer* (New York: Hawthorn, 1965), 56.
4. Ibid., 58.

5. Albert Schweitzer *The Animal World of Albert Schweitzer*, ed. and trans. Charles R. Joy (Boston: Beacon Press, 1950), 19.

6. Ibid., 20.

7. Ibid., 21.

8. Frederick Franck, *My Days with Albert Schweitzer* (New York: Lyons & Burford, 1959), 27.

9. Ibid., 31.

10. Ibid., 289.

11. Anderson, *The Schweitzer Album*, 114.

12. Norman Cousins, ed., *The Words of Albert Schweitzer* (New York: Newmarket Press, 1984), 95–96.

13. George Marshall and David Poling, *Schweitzer: A Biography* (Garden City, New York: Doubleday, 1971), 238.

14. Ibid., 218.

15. Ibid., 68.

16. Albert Schweitzer, *Memoirs of Childhood and Youth*, trans. C. T. Campion (New York: Macmillan, 1958), 45.

17. Marshall and Poling, *Schweitzer: A Biography*, 277.

18. Albert Schweitzer, *On the Edge of the Primeval Forest* and *More from the Primeval Forest*, trans. C. T. Campion (New York: Macmillan, 1948), 116–18.

19. Montague, *The Why of Albert Schweitzer*, 10.

20. Marshall and Poling, *Schweitzer: A Biography*, 305.

Chapter 10: A Good Shepherd's Testimony

1. George Marshall and David Poling, *Schweitzer: A Biography* (Garden City, NY: Doubleday, 1971), 306.

2. Ibid.

3. Joseph Franklin Montague, *The Why of Albert Schweitzer* (New York: Hawthorn, 1965), 109–10.

4. Ibid., 134.

5. Marshall and Poling, *Schweitzer: A Biography*, 239.

6. Ibid., 293.

7. Donald Desfor, Louise Jilek-Aal, and Marvin Meyer, "Albert Schweitzer at Lambaréné: A Photographic Essay," paras.

11–14, in *Finding Lambaréné* (Orange, CA: Chapman University, Albert Schweitzer Institute, 2007).

8. Marshall and Poling, *Schweitzer: A Biography*, 307–8.

Afterword

1. Albert Schweitzer, *Memoirs of Childhood and Youth*, trans. C. T. Campion (New York: Macmillan, 1958), 67–68.

2. Albert Schweitzer Fellowship (ASF), "Why 'Beyond Boulders'?" Beyond Boulders: Blog, http:// schweitzerfellowship.wordpress.com/why-beyond-boulders/.

3. Albert Schweitzer Fellowship, http://www .schweitzerfellowship.org/features/who/mission.aspx.

4. Albert Schweitzer Fellowship, http://www .schweitzerfellowship.org/features/lamb/hosp.aspx.

5. Ibid.

6. Joseph Franklin Montague, *The Why of Albert Schweitzer* (New York: Hawthorn, 1965).

Appendix 1

1. Albert Schweitzer, *Memoirs of Childhood and Youth*, trans. C. T. Campion (New York: Macmillan, 1958), 66.

2. From *Epilogue*, cited in *Albert Schweitzer: An Anthology*, ed. by Charles R. Joy (Boston: Beacon Press, 1947), 295.

3. From *Reverence for Life*, cited in ibid., 248.

4. Albert Schweitzer, *Reverence for Life* (New York: Harper & Row, 1969), 59.

5. Albert Schweitzer, *The Teaching of Reverence for Life*, trans. Richard Winston and Clara Winston (New York: Holt, Rinehart, & Winston, 1965), 41.

6. From *Christianity and the Religions of the World*, cited in *Albert Schweitzer: An Anthology*, 78.

7. Albert Schweitzer, *The Mysticism of Paul the Apostle* (New York: Macmillan, 1960), 378.

8. Albert Schweitzer, *Christianity and the Religions of the World* (London: Allen & Unwin, 1960), 82.

9. Ibid., 82–83.

10. Norman Cousins, ed., *The Words of Albert Schweitzer* (New York: Newmarket Press, 1984), 54.

11. "The One-Talent People," *Christian Herald*, September 1949, 64.

Appendix 3

1. To view the complete Albert Schweitzer Hospital Charter of Values, visit the Albert Schweitzer Fellowship website: Albert Schweitzer Fellowship, http://www.schweitzerfellowship.org/features/lamb/hosp_mission.aspx.

Selected Bibliography

Albert Schweitzer Fellowship. Charter of Values. http://www
.schweitzerfellowship.org/features/lamb/hosp_mission.aspx.
———. "Why 'Beyond Boulders?'" Beyond Boulders: Blog. http://
schweitzerfellowship.wordpress.com/why-beyond-boulders/.
Anderson, Erica. *The Schweitzer Album*. New York: Harper & Row, 1965.
Bahr, Hans Walter, ed. *Albert Schweitzer Letters, 1905–1965*. Trans.
Joachim Neugroschel. New York: Macmillan, 1992.
Clark, Henry. *The Ethical Mysticism of Albert Schweitzer*. Boston: Beacon
Press, 1962.
Cousins, Norman, ed. *The Words of Albert Schweitzer*. New York:
Newmarket Press, 1984.
Desfor, Donald, Louise Jilek-Aall, and Marvin Meyer. *Finding Lambaréné*.
Orange, CA: Chapman University, Albert Schweitzer Institute, 2007.
Franck, Frederick. *My Days with Albert Schweitzer*. New York: Lyons &
Burford, 1959.
Marshall, George, and David Poling. *Schweitzer: A Biography*. Garden City,
NY: Doubleday, 1971.
Montague, Joseph Franklin. *The Why of Albert Schweitzer*. New York:
Hawthorn, 1965.
Schweitzer, Albert. *The Animal World of Albert Schweitzer*. Edited and
trans. Charles R. Joy. Boston: Beacon Press, 1950.
———. *Memoirs of Childhood and Youth*. trans. C. T. Campion. New York:
Macmillan, 1958.
———. *On the Edge of the Primeval Forest* and *More from the Primeval Forest*.
trans. C. T. Campion. New York: Macmillan, 1948.
———. *Out of My Life and Thought: An Autobiography*. trans. C. T.
Campion. New York: Henry Holt, 1933.
Note: In addition to the notes, the author has used information from
the above books and sites to write facts and insights on Schweitzer's life and
work throughout this book.

About the Author

Ken Gire is the author of more than a dozen books. He has won two Gold Medallion awards. His four-book "Moments with the Savior" series has sold more than 250,000 copies. A full-time writer and speaker, Ken has been involved in the ministries of Young Life, Insight for Living, and Reflective Living. He presently lives in Baltimore, Maryland.